Blessed With Beauty For Ashes

The Power of Godly Perseverance

Sandra E. E. Williams

Disclaimers

This is based on a true story. The names and identifying details have been changed to protect the privacy of individuals.

I have tried to recreate events, locales and conversations from my memories of them. In order to maintain their anonymity in some instances I have changed the names of individuals and places, I may have changed some identifying characteristics and details such as physical properties, occupations and place or residence.

Although the author and publisher have made every effort to ensure that the information in this book was correct at press time, the author and publisher do not assume and hereby disclaim any liability to any party for any loss, damage, or disruption caused by errors or omissions, whether such errors or omissions result from negligence, accident or any other cause.

Copyright © 2019 by Sandra E. E. Williams

Sandra E. E. Williams Publishing

Books@Blessedwithbeautyforashes.com

Scripture taken from the New King James Version®. Copyright © 1982 by Thomas Nelson. Used by permission. All rights reserved.

Book Cover Design by The Book Cover Whisperer: ProfessionalBookCoverDesign.com

All rights reserved. No part of this publication may be reproduced, stored in a retrieval system, or transmitted in any form or by any means- electronic, mechanical, digital, photocopy, recording or any other-except for brief quotations in printed review, without the prior written permission of the publisher.

ISBN – 978-0-578-47337-6

Printed in the Unites States of America

Preface

Life as I knew it was over. I was instantly and suddenly left alone in the world to face everything and everyone on my own. I felt as if my very soul was separated from life. How could this have happened, why did this happen oh God? The pain I felt was so intense that I became numb, until I looked at my two beautiful girls and knew I had to be there for them. I had to beg my heavenly father to give me strength to continue day by day until I was able to get my mind wrapped around what had taken place and what had to be done. Mom was gone and her insensitive brothers were overseeing the funeral arrangements as if I never existed. They behaved as if they were burying their dead and I was a necessary annoyance that had to attend. Mom and I had started to build our dream house, and while she was dying, her brothers were trying to take the house. They tried to take the house, even more intensely after she passed. They plotted to steal our dream and live comfortably off of our hard work. The death of a close loved one always brings out peoples true colors. I tried to figure out in my head, at which point did they begin to hate me. Was it during the summers I spent at their Caribbean homes with their kids? Was it when they came to visit me in my home in the States or during our family vacations, or was it as my mother and I began dreaming big and executing the documented dream strategy? It's a little scary to find out you have enemies and that your enemies are within your family without you even knowing it… never the less God's plan will always prevail. This is a story of my journey and perseverance through various challenges in my life. This true story exemplifies how I stood on God's promises; that he would never leave me alone and he would give me life and life more abundantly if you trust and believe.

Chapter 1

With excitement, the girls and I anxiously packed our bathing suits and flips flops in anticipation of jumping into the crystal clear waters of the Caribbean and rubbing the white sand through our freshly pedicured toes. My Mom was busy at the house preparing all of our favorite fruits and foods, waiting for her girls to land on the island for two fabulous weeks.

…We looked out of the window as the plane flew over the northwest side of the island to line up with the runway on the north side of the island. We were able to identify familiar houses and land marks as we got closer and closer to landing. Once I stepped off the plane and took a deep breath I did a little happy dance, and then we were off to immigration and then customs. It seemed like it took forever to get our bags, when finally I saw familiar bags on the luggage belt. Now we were off to pick up the rental car. We had so many things with us, and as traditional Island people, we just have to bring everything from America to our home country for everybody. It's just a part of the culture. Things like food, toiletries and clothes are so much cheaper and readily available in America. I was excited to give Mom her pretty dresses we had picked out just for her. I couldn't wait to see her try them on and look in the mirror. We were going to go driving all around the island, go to beach, visit family and friends, eat, eat and eat some more. We were going to hang out with each other and enjoy one another's company.

As we pulled up in the driveway, Mom was looking out of the window and said in her nice soft spoken voice....ahhhh my babies are here. Hi sweetheart she said in a way only she could say it. There were hugs and kisses as we went into the house. The girls ran to their rooms as I looked all around the place and then I turned and noticed my Mom looked different. Her eyes, her weight loss, something was not right…

Years ago Mom had decided to return to her home country, Grenada. The island where land and sea make beauty. I wanted her to stay in America where she had lived for so many years. We were used to going to see her all the time and just picking up the phone and calling whenever we wanted. Tiffany, my oldest daughter, called her Grandmom every day after school to give the blow by blow of the day and to get help with her homework, especially math. Nina, my youngest daughter, enjoyed all of the loving up and spoiling her

Grandmom would give her, but Mom wanted to leave the cold weather and go to the sunshine. We talked about how she would sustain herself comfortably and still do the things she liked to do like evangelism and traveling. We spoke about the piece of land she always talked about, that her brother promised her for a wedding gift in the 1960's. We went on to have a fabulous vacation but in the back of my mind I kept thinking I did not like the way my Mom looked. She just did not look well. She told me she was fine and I left it like that for the time being.

When the girls and I returned home to the States, my Mom told me she contacted her brother in Saint Croix and asked if he was still willing to give her the land. He gladly answered my Mom and said of course, anything for my favorite sister. She called me all excited of what we could and would do with the land that he promised her. However at that specific point in time, no true planning had occurred. I looked at a few sketches and house plans trying to put something informal together, but I really didn't pursue with eagerness at that time.

Months had gone by since I last thought about the dream house, and while sleeping one night I had an out of body experience. A dream that God woke me up from my deep sleep and began to speak to me about this house in Belmont, Granada. He called me by name, he said Sandra, and my spirit got up and stood with him and I began to talk with my heavenly father. I could see myself lying in the bed and yet I was standing and having a conversation about this land in Grenada with the Spirit of God. We talked about me building and how I needed to build it and I needed to begin. The scripture

Isiah 48:17 was given to me. I am the Lord your God who teaches you to profit, who leads you by the way you should go. Right after the conversation he gave me a hug and a kiss. Strangely enough immediately after the Spirit of God left the kiss became perverted, which made me think the whole thing was strange and perhaps it was a dream as opposed to an actual experience, vision, or encounter with the Spirit of the Living God. This was a trick of the enemy to have me question my encounter with God. (I understood this concept from a pastor I listen to on a regular basis.) When I laid back in the bed, my spirit that is, I began to speak in tongues. I questioned myself for days and then temporarily dismissed it. I mentioned the dream to my Mother and she just said it was Gods favor upon me, and to remember my dream.

Weeks passed and I forgot all about the dream until I was watching a show on TV about renting houses while on vacation. It's interesting how God sends confirmation and little reminders and situations that nudge your mind. I later asked my now ex-husband about how does one go about obtaining land in the Caribbean, specifically in Grenada. He said it was difficult and hard for people to buy land. He said it's not an easy thing to do and you should just forget about that idea. I later realized that was not true at all. Now that I reflect back on that conversation, I ask myself, why did I ask him when my mother and I had already had our discussion some time ago about the land gifted from her brother. Later in the same year one of my best friends came to visit me from Grenada and we had a conversation about buying land and building houses. She spoke about how she and her husband were in the process of purchasing land and expressed how simple it was to obtain land and then at that exact moment I remembered the dream.

Chapter 2

I called my Mom later that week and we once again spoke about the land promised to my Mom by my Uncle Cornelius and how we should proceed. Through research I discovered all of the agencies on the island that needed to be involved in building a house from the ground up. I researched where the blue prints had to be approved, the land survey department, who sold concrete blocks, concrete, plywood, sand, stone, steel etc.

I needed to purposefully sketch a draft blue print plan and determine the size of the house based on the shape and size of the land. I looked through countless books and house plans to get ideas. I took one or two ideas from each plan I selected and then added my personal creativity. My mother's brother, Cornelius often spoke to both my mother and me about where we were in the process of the house. At one point my Uncle Cornelius asked if I had ever thought about having an apartment as part of the plan since many people in the Caribbean build an apartment as part of a house for income. I thought that was a great idea and ran with it…

In the midst of outlining this dream house on paper, I interestingly enough was never overtaken by how this journey was going to be funded. It was almost an impossible and unimaginable goal to achieve, but I had this unexplainable drive rooted deep within me to move forward.

From various people I personally knew on the island and throughout the world, I obtained a few estimates for a formal blue print and building plan. I researched having a plan drawn in the United States to be used in the Caribbean but that was quickly shot down. In the Caribbean or at least in Grenada a house plan must be officially finalized at a minimum by a local licensed and certified architect. I was told, even if I had the plan drawn in the United States an Architect in Grenada would have to re-draw it …ahhhh. That would be double money, and so I was left to finding a local architect on the island. I had heard from various people that house plans can cost thousands and even tens of thousands.

My Mother was an integral part of this process. She knew so many people that were talented in many areas. One of my Mother's church member's son, Tyrone Taylor, was just beginning his architect business and had agreed to work with me on the design of the house for a reasonable price, based on the current market. Although this was challenging for me, it was a good and fair price.

Tyrone also agreed to take his payments in installments because of my Mom. The overall price of the plan and the building of the house seemed so unmanageable but I decided to look at it in manageable pieces. I broke down the building project into phases. The phases had sub phases that could then become more manageable.

The building of the house was broken down into these phases:

1. Design and payment of blue print
2. Approval of blue prints
3. Purchase of aggregated materials
4. Foundation
5. Concrete floor & Roughing
6. Walls/Electrical & plumbing conduits
7. Ring beam
8. Roof

9. Plastering

10. Windows/Doors

11. Painting

12. Floor Tile

13. Light fixtures

14. Bathroom tile & fixtures

15. Kitchen cabinets

16. Miscellaneous

17. Furniture & appliances

18. Garage

19. Landscaping

20. Fencing

The breaking down of the project into these phases prevented me from becoming overwhelmed. I looked at it similarly to how I look at completing a rubrics cube. I break it into logical pieces I am able to handle. I may not be quick, but I am able to solve the cube.

As this process really began to kick off, I thought since I got favor with the drawing of the plan, God was opening doors for this to really move forward. I met with Tyrone, the architect, a few times and then spoke to him many many times on the phone once I returned to America regarding the details of the blue print.

The plan Tyrone drew included electrical, plumbing, roofing and the foundation…. layer after layer of blue prints. The shape and slope of the land determined the layout of the house. Prior to working with him, I had no idea a blue print involved that much. A saturation test of the land was also conducted by Tyrone to determine the rate of absorption and some other types of technical test such as the depth of the bedrock etc. Well, well, what a process I thought.

In hindsight and reflecting on the past, these details bring tears to my eyes. When I think of the times I wrote out all of the details required to be documented, hour after hour, day after day, month after month and year after year, I just give thanks for the ability and strength. The thought of working so hard on so many levels of this project and the hatred I had to face from people who wanted to just take everything from me and who hated me because of a dream,….. I have to sit and shake my head in disbelief………..

The amount of hatred that grew from this project from family members that could have enjoyed this moment in unison with me, my Mom and our family was just too much for me at the time. I thought I was going to lose my mind…..

Getting back to the building process; Building Control Authority, BCA is where everything begins officially with the inception of building any building structure in Grenada. A building permit had to be obtained with a licensed contractor, electrician and plumber. The first speed bump was the fact that the land was not yet transferred into my Mom's name from her brother. BCA insisted we have a legal document to state the status of the land. This document would prove to be invaluable as time goes by. It was actually God working in the background to protect the vision and dream he had put into my heart. The document was very specific and was overseen by a lawyer and notary, at a cost of course.

Per BCA, the legal and binding document had to be rewritten three times until it was exactly to their liking. They stated it had to be very specific in case there were any legal issues in the future about ownership, since we were not able to pick up the house and place it on another piece of land.

As time went on, I often questioned why it was taking so long to transfer the land. I became upset as the money passed through my hands towards the project and yet the land ownership was not finalized. At one point I even questioned if I had heard right from God and that perhaps I should just go and pay for an issue free and legally clear piece of land without dealing with this nonsense from my Uncle Cornelius. It's funny how you want to tell God how your dream should be completed and the route it should take as if he can't possibly be right about the path required to complete a task, assignment or in this case a dream.

I mentioned this concern to my Mom numerous times. She was so protective of her brother. She was the big sister defending her brother's character. Mom repeatedly assured me that her brother would follow through with his promise, and not to worry since his word has always been good and he would not lie to her ever. Something just kept gnawing at me with regards to this statement but I just couldn't put my finger on it. I took my deep breath and we moved along with the building process for the time being.

Once the plan was approved by BCA, the next phase was to search for someone to build this house and to find out how much would it cost. Once again I refused to look at the overall cost as some mountain I could not climb. This was where I dove further into planning, writing my thoughts, and juggling funds. I creatively came up with ways to fund the project like obtaining a vendors business license to sell goods, nationally and internationally as well as attend various flea markets.

I spoke with my then brother in law who lived in Dominica. He built his house and many others on that island and was extremely creative and gifted with construction and ideas for building. Dominicans are known for their building skills as that particular island is very mountainous. So it was decided that my brother in law was going to build the house, or at least that was the plan at the time.

Mom and I calculated and estimated the cost of each of the four major phases; foundation, floor, walls, and roof, and discussed creatively how we would fund it.

This was our individual and collective dream project to have a serious revenue stream and allow her to travel all over the world while evangelizing just like she wanted to do. This would make both of our lives much easier financially, and we were in it together. She could retire in complete comfort and I would have a Caribbean home where my children and friends could enjoy as well. We could fund school bags and uniforms for children in the village etc. with the additional income. I was beyond excited. All of my thoughts and ideas were associated with building the house every single day. It had taken over my life.

I was at the local hardware store everyday window shopping and purchasing the things on the list I received from the builder every chance I got. I was in the hardware store so often they knew me by sight and by name. Doors were being opened by God for unprecedented favor with companies and individuals. I made payment arrangements with the masonry companies for concrete and concrete blocks in Grenada. I also made payment arrangements with businesses for steel, (rebar) and form ply. I made it a point to learn as much as possible and be involved with everything about building, down to the pounds needed for the concrete and wood nails. Every single penny counted. I oversaw everything as I was fully immersed in this project. I carried brown bag lunches and left overs every day from home to assist with saving as well. I was being taught step by step on how to complete the goal.

The house was artistically designed to have multiple units. One housing unit would be for Mom to live in and the other remaining housing unit to be rented weekly to tourist for residual income. I sometimes worked "on-call" at my job when I was an Analyst and saved as much money as I possibly could from the "on call" role. I loved my Mom so much and wanted to make sure my Mom was as comfortable as she deserved to be during the latter part of her life.

I also saved money by participating in a long time Caribbean practice called box, hand, box hand, Su Su or meeting turn. The name of this practice was based on the specific island in the Caribbean. This has been a form of savings in the Caribbean for hundreds of years. Many West Indians participate in this type of savings to go on vacation, make large purchases, pay bills off etc. Some people say these types of old island savings methods don't work and I am sure they have examples of when it did not work for them, but in this case, box hand has helped pay for many things towards this house project. My paternal Grandmother never had the opportunity to go to secondary school and yet she was brilliant. She used this mechanism to purchase a piece of land for all of her children. My father often tells me the stories of him taking his mother's box hand to be paid on a weekly basis, when he was a youngster. This process can be done weekly or monthly depending on the set up of that particular "box hand".

I purchased the initial PVC pipes used for the foundation and roughing in the concrete floor in the U.S. and had them shipped, cleared and stored in Grenada. (If I had this to do all over I would not ship these pipes again.) The steel, concrete, blocks, nails everything else needed at this point was purchased on island and ready to begin with regards to building materials. After I saved what was estimated to be needed for the labor of the foundation, we were ready to break ground and begin. I could barely contain myself. We were finally ready to actually see the reality of the dream begin! We were ready to break ground in November of 1999.

My Mom moved back to the States for a period of time shortly before the foundation began. She said she would return to Grenada at some point and I thought great, that would give us enough time to save and build before she was ready to return again to the island.

Chapter 3

The house was moving along, things were going a little bumpy and money was needed every day. The stress was unbelievably high. The concrete in the foundation was poured in November of 1999 and shortly after the concrete was poured we received the news about the hurricane that was in the Caribbean. Oh my goodness, I could not believe it. I just purchased a truck load of sand and gravel as well as a water tank and a hurricane was on its way. Marvin, my now ex-husband, the kids, my Mom and I all went out to dinner in Jenkintown, NJ the night the hurricane hit the island. It was a long dinner and a long night. We chatted and laughed and so on, well into the evening. I thought to myself how could God allow me to begin this project that we spoke about and the hurricane is coming to blow everything away. Mom spoke to her brother Cornelius who by the way lives on the island of Saint Croix, about the foundation being poured and the impending hurricane. (Sometimes it bothered me that they chatted so much about everything since no one else was helping with funding the project. Why did he or any of her other brothers need an update if none of them were providing any financial assistance.) Moving along, Uncle Cornelius spoke to Mom quite frequently, his favorite sister as he would say. He mentioned to her that when he was pouring the foundation for his house a hurricane hit as well.

Hurricane Jose was on its way. The hurricane winds blew and blew and I paced and paced up and down throughout the night. My Mom said, Sandra relax. Just know that the water tank is probably in St Kitts by now, ha ha ha she said and the sand is just gone. She said God will give the resources for you to get the materials again.

    I fell asleep that night trying to visualize what had occurred during the storm and wanted it to be over. Daylight seemed so far away as I slipped into a deep sleep. As soon as my eyes opened the next morning I tried several times to contact everyone I knew on the island to check on them and I also called the builder to hear the news about the foundation. My breath stopped as he answered the phone, I was so glad to hear his voice. I stuttered saying… oh I am so glad you answered…how is everything? Have you been able to see what happened up at the house? He said he was at the house first thing that morning. He said Sandra it was as if the wind had hands. The black 6 ft. water tank was originally not full and the wind appeared to have unscrewed the lid of the tank and the tank stayed put and filled up with water, giving it weight. The sand was there as well but very wet. I was in shock! It knew it could have only been God that had done this, it was God that allowed the supplies to remain untouched and not harmed. My confidence and faith in God grew with that hurricane. I knew beyond a doubt that this was indeed an order and plan by God for this house to be built for a purpose and as a testimony, only I had no idea how much of a testimony at the time.

The project came to a close after the foundation was completed. I needed to regroup and save for the floor which would be very expensive. When Mom was still in the States and preparing to move to Grenada again, I was desperately trying to make sure this house was completed either before she got down there or shortly after. I was so concerned about where she would live and how she would go to the store and so on. Why did she want to go back or have to go back down there permanently to live so soon? I had envisioned her always living in the States and then going to the house from time to time, however she was ready to go and the house was nowhere near ready. I questioned God and asked how can this be. Mom is ready to go back to Grenada and that was not my plan. "You oh God said this would be completed at some point". What was going on I wondered. Imagine I was telling God when this project should be completed.

In the meantime my Mom had moved to Grenada and was staying with another brother, Jerome. Why did my Mom think it was okay to stay with her brother and his family? I thought this brother had truly loved her and me. I had fond memories for the most part with this brother named Jerome. Nothing had prepared me for what was ahead with my mother's brothers, absolutely nothing.

Thankfully Mom quickly found a nice place in Fairhill a few weeks after she was on the island, which is not a bad section of the island to live. My daughter Tiffany went and spent the summer with her Grandmom that year, which was a memorable time for both of them. They had great memories. Prior to Mom leaving to go to Grenada she truly believed her brother, in Grenada, would help her with whatever she needed…truly believed it. I never understood her unwavering belief in him, who she thought could not do wrong. (I'm not sure I will ever understand it either, especially when the upcoming years prove otherwise.) He did not always have the characteristics of an honest person. I remember the good times and it was not always this bad, however as time went on it was unbearable. My Mom always insisted he was never guilty of any wrong doing. We had several deep discussions about not trusting him and she would get very upset and defend two of the three of her brothers. Two of my mother's brothers lived in the Caribbean and one lived in Oklahoma, (he has another story that could be a short story in of itself).

My Mom lived off of her pension and social security, and I managed her bank accounts in the States. She hated dealing with the bank and bills. Every month I would send her requested amount of money and her bank statement. She never liked banks and never wanted to deal with them so I managed and paid all of her bills since I turned 18, after my Mom and dad officially divorced. My dad used to be the one in the household that handled the bills when they were married and she just never liked dealing with it since then. Mom decided to open an account in Grenada and she added her brother to her account there since she still did not like banks, only she managed her money there. The island is small and at some point everybody knows somebody that knows somebody. I knew my Uncle Jerome wanted to know everything about my mother's finances and I mentioned to her that she should not have him of all people on her account and she insisted he would not do anything with the account and was upset I even mentioned it. I just love my mother, I love my mother, bless her heart. When she passed he took everything out of her account and kept it for himself.

The next phase of the house will prove to be a turning point in the relationship between my mother's brothers and myself. I saved for two years to get enough money for the concrete floor, and the inside concrete cistern. As usual, I was beyond excited about building when the construction was about to start up again. My Mom was getting older and I was just getting nervous and wondering how she would be able to take care of herself in another country without me. I asked everyday if she ate and what she did that day and so on. I felt that she was not telling me how things really went. I knew she would ask a friend of mine to pick up water for her from time to time. My mother no longer drove at this time and her precious brother was too busy to assist her. My Mom became pastor of the Walton church in Black Rock, Grenada, and she was in her element. She loved to pastor and had a huge heart for people. However some people were not happy with her appointment since they did not believe females should oversee a church.

After the installing of the concrete floor, and while the builder was filling in the foundation I received a phone call. The builder stated he believed another apartment could be incorporated into the building. I said okay and agreed to not fill in the bottom section of the structure, to make room for yet another apartment. A few months later, I flew to Grenada to see what was going on and make a final determination of the next steps. My Mom and I walked the property and prayed over it while thanking God for reaching this stage. I could see that an apartment towards the back of the property could really be done. It was as if I could actually visualize the final product. The ground on that side of the property was primarily stone, so the giant rocks below the floor would need to be chipped and removed by hand since the walls were partially up around this area. This is how the second apartment for the house was created. My Mom said to me why don't you ask your Uncle to look at it so he could feel included. I frowned and asked her which uncle and she said your Uncle Jerome since he is here on the island, he could help you. Now how could he help me and why would I include him since it was all of my money that was being spent. He was not giving any money and only wanted to give advice on something he himself had never done. He had never built a sizable house himself or successfully participated in the building of one with his money. Ahhhh I love my mother, I love my mother, bless her heart.

I called my Uncle Jerome and asked him if he knew of an electrician and he seemed excited to get the call, (SMH) and told me of some electrician that he had used in some past projects for the church and some parishioners. I said okay and contacted the electrician. The referred electrician came up to the house to see the job that needed to be done. He called me and gave me an outrageous price. Simultaneously another electrician of my choice was at the site a few minutes before the referred electrician, to also give me an estimate. Within that same week I thanked the electrician my Uncle Jerome recommended for giving me the estimate, after fussing and venting with my Mom, and told him his services would not be needed. This electrician tried to charge me Six thousand dollars MORE than other electricians I received estimates from to complete the work. The referred electrician went back up to the house where the workmen were working and fussed and cuss off the people up there, to the point where the builder picked up the phone and called me stating he would quit if I hire this man. This was just simply embarrassing……. He was most definitely not getting the job for sure and how could my Uncle refer such a mad man, chupzzzz. (This is a colloquial habit, the sucking of the teeth, identified as chupzzzz)

Chapter 4

My mother's brother from Saint Croix was on the island shortly after that electrician fiasco incident for a wedding, and decided to go up to the house in Belmont to check it out. He became very upset that the house was so large and could not believe the size. He contacted me and asked why is the house so big. Keep in mind the land has not been transferred as yet. I said to my mother please ask your brother about the transfer and that I will pay for the transfer at this point. This is not a good position to be in since tens of thousands of dollars have already been spent and family was involved etc. My mother continued to state and profess her brother will transfer the land because he said it and would never lie. Imagine this high belief in the brothers that they can never do wrong. At this point I would be the one that would lose financially and where would my Mom live once she left the mason house that she lived in at this time? I felt like I was under so much pressure. Mean time I had two children and a worthless husband that felt like an adult leach on me. He worked on and off and was abusive. I was trying to figure out how to get out of my marriage. How did I get into this madness? I supported the house hold and he had found someone to take care of him in America. He would constantly tell me who else would want you, look at you and how you look so terrible. I began to take the long way home and would sit outside of the house before I even entered. Whenever he walked into the room I was in, I would just tighten up. How did it get to this point? My father even told me at some time or the other that he would help me put him out. I even stopped going to events with my family and friends because of him. Marvin told me we should only be separated when I have to go to work. He wanted to control every hour of my day outside of work. He would bring women to the house when I was at work and tell me they were just friends. We had one vehicle at first and I was stuck in the house with the kids when he went to his weekend job with the car 45 minutes away. If I wanted the car I had to take him to work with the kids in the car and pick him up on time. If I was even 3 minutes late he would yell at me for making him stand out front of the office like an idiot he would say. How dare you are late for me. Keep in mind this was my vehicle that I paid for…. Ahhhh take a deep breath… I'm getting carried away. I told him to catch the bus and he did for a while and then he fussed so much I literally could not take it anymore and I would just take him to get him out of the house. He worked on Sundays and said there was no need for me to go to church since there was nothing church could do for me. I was just so disgusted with him and his crap.

One day I looked at Marvin while sitting in the living room and tried to figure out what did I ever see in this person. I remember crying in my sleep at night trying to figure out how could this really be my life and wondering if this was how it was going to be for the rest of my life. This situation had to change. I remember "having a 30 day menstrual cycle on purpose" for most of the calendar year if you know what I mean. I slept with a maxi pad every night and promised him I would see a physician to see what was wrong. ☺ Chupzzzz that was an appointment that would never happen as far as I was concerned. I went as far as hiring a realtor to sell the house, my house, to get Marvin out. I had asked him to leave and he said the only way he would leave would be if the police took him out. This went on for years. I felt stuck with no way out.

One Sunday Marvin took the vehicle and I took a trolley, a train and a bus to go to church with the kids. I just had to go. I begged God to get me out of my situation. I got into this situation against my mother's wishes and definitely not the way God would have approved and I felt as though this was my punishment. I had already had a daughter when I met Marvin and then had another with him. I never introduced him as my husband or even called him my husband, just Marvin. I would say this is Marvin and these are my children Tiffany and Nina. It was not all bad but it was bad most of the time. Whenever I got behind in the mortgage and asked him for help he would say "if I wasn't here you would still have to find a way to pay, so I'm not the problem". When he would give me money towards the house I would have to hear how he saved the house. Imagine that he said he saved the house that he lived in and didn't contribute to financially on a regular basis. I felt like I was losing my mind.

I took the kids to Grenada to spend Easter with my Mom and was so happy to be away from him. When I got to my Moms, she asked me if I was going to call him to tell him I had arrived….why would I do that. I was glad to be away. So my Mom being my Mom gave him a call on behalf of me to say that the kids and I arrived safely and then gave me the phone. I said hello and he asked if I was going to call…I never responded and said see you in two weeks.

Upon my return, two weeks later, I found a nice gold bracelet in the back guest bedroom in the bed. I kept the bracelet since I liked it and just planned to get him out of my house and life. This is where the contract with the realtor comes into play. I had planned on moving out of the house with the kids into another place on my own and move back into my home when Marvin moved out. LOL that's how bad I wanted to get out of the situation. At that time he had worked for the airline and I would occasionally get tickets from him to fly here and there until he told me I had reach his established quota for me to fly on his privileges. Even though he was on my medical, dental and vision insurance and used them to the fullest.

For all of the reasons previously mentioned I was amazed when he Marvin went around telling people how much he loved me when I put him out. Ha ha ha ha ha ha ha. I could not stop laughing at his nerve. He told all kinds of lies on me to get me to take him back but that day would never happen in this life or life after.

I no longer included Marvin in any discussions of the house since he was only interested in the topic whenever someone visited us and asked about the house. I would just shake my head in amazement and disgust. It was a matter of time before he was fully out of the home and in my mind he was no longer relevant.

I remember when for the 5th or 6th time I had asked Marvin to leave the home, he actually stated he wanted to go to counseling. I could not even imagine this line of thinking from him. He started going to church with me but could not sit in the church. He would sweat during the preaching and have to leave out of the service. He kept saying he wanted to go to counseling but I was past that point. I told him only people that are interested in saving a marriage want to go to counseling and since I am no longer interested, there is no longer a need for me to go. I had left him emotionally long ago. One day I just got fed up of being fed up and packed up all of his things and put them by in garbage bags by the door. I told him he had 30 days to get out. The time before that, perhaps somewhere around the 4th time, I postponed his somewhat eviction since he had lost his job. I could not believe the man had lost his job and I had compassion and kept my imminent eviction of him from my life to myself. I never shared my plan with anyone because I did not want anything to stop my plan. This time was different, he had to go and the clock had started ticking.

Moving right along…….

I was so happy when he left and he could not understand why I was so happy and at peace. The girls and I went out to dinner to celebrate when he left. He was so pitiful that he took the iron and laundry detergent when he left and told me he purchased it. Well if that is what it took for him to hit the road then take it. I didn't have money at the time to buy laundry detergent or an iron until the next pay day but I was able to work it out creatively.

Chapter 5

During the Easter visit with my Mom I noticed she looked much slimmer than the last time I saw her. I asked her if she was okay and she said she was, but I kept my thoughts to myself and wondered. During the vacation I had to look for another builder since Marvin and I were on the rocks and his brother was not so inclined to build the house anymore. One of the Walton Holiness part time pastors was recommended to me by my Mom and I agreed for him to continue the project for a period of time. In the meantime my Mom called her brother to find out about the status of the transfer for the land. The transfer cost would have been roughly 12,000 CBD dollars at this point. I was even willing to pay for the transfer to speed things along and to get out of the tangled web with my Uncle. He kept saying he was going to transfer the land but just kept stalling. Once I found a new contractor in Grenada, I was ready to go up with the walls of the house.

Meantime I still had the nerve to ask Marvin for a plane ticket to go and see my Mom and just hang out for the long weekend. This time when I went to see my Mom, I was stunned. She had lost a great deal of weight and I knew something was majorly wrong. I went back again a few weeks later to not only check on the progress of the house but to see what was going on with my Mom again. I took the kids with me this time and my nightmare just kept continuing. How could my mother be so sick and not say anything. Did anyone else see how much weight she was losing?

I was unknowingly about to enter one of the darkest seasons of my life. My Mom's weight loss was no longer something that could be ignored or not discussed, as it had become a serious situation. I was not sure what was medically wrong but I desperately needed my mother to come to America to see her physician. I pleaded with her to see a physician until she said to me if I ask her one more time she is going to leave the house until my vacation is over and then return back to her home. My mouth dropped open because of the push back and defensive mode Mom had taken with me, of all people. I asked myself how come no one has noticed this weight loss except me, how come no one else is saying Pastor Nelson or sister etc. what is going on with you? I had been calling everyone asking them how she looked. I would call her and ask her if she ate and what she ate. I could not let this go. Tiffany begged me to not ask her Grandmom anymore but I could not let it go, I had to make sure my Mother was taken care of and was seen by someone soon. I pushed this issue and asked her brother if he is not noticing her weight loss, and he said to me nothing is wrong, that he is not seeing anything different, chupzzzz. I thought to myself this man is a true idiot.

A friend of mine from my Mom's church even called me one Sunday and told me my Mom had fainted in church and I called her about the incident. She was clearly annoyed and wanted to know who told me and that they should not have told me as oppose to looking at the fact that I was concerned. I, who am off island, can see that something is wrong and the brother and friends on island are not seeing anything wrong; why is that?

Chapter 6

Back in Grenada again. I was going to the island at least twice a month at this point, using free tickets for me and the girls, from Marvin. A very good friend of mine rented a vehicle for me and the girls and I picked it up at the airport. We were so happy to get to the island for a little peace and quiet but I so wanted to see my Mom and find out how she was doing. I suspected she was not telling me everything and I wanted to see her for myself. Perhaps I should not have asked for tickets from Marvin but then I thought why not. He had been a terror in my life but it was not all of his fault since he only did what I ultimately permitted. At this point in time I was certainly not perfect at all and somehow had lost my scruples with regards to that marriage. The walls of my life were beginning to crumble all around me and I needed an escape.

A year or so prior Aunt Adeline, my Mom's only sister had passed away from uterine cancer. I remember my Mom and me visiting her sister in the States and Mom saying, for me to let her know if she ever becomes cantankerous like her sister. We talked about if someone had cancer was it better to go through the treatment and suffer or live out your life until the cancer took you. That conversation would always resonate with me and was brought back to my memory at this exact moment.

I had to make all of the funeral arrangements for my aunt's funeral. I found out, in tremendous detail by trying to help out the family, so much about burying someone. No one wanted to deal with my aunt's funeral and my mother was in Grenada when her sister's death occurred. As a preacher's kid I had been to hundreds of funerals and sat in the back of the church doing homework, but this was different. I helped my cousins and mother because my mother did not want her sisters body donated to science since no funds were coming in from all of my aunt's six children. The family and extended family pooled money together for the funeral. 18 months later another funeral would unknowingly have to be planned………

I could not understand why my Mom was so secretive about her illness, but I just prayed and asked God to have her to come the States to see what was going on with her. Thankfully she agreed and I made the flight arrangements and was so happy to pick her up from the airport. I made the doctor appointment for Mom prior to her arrival to the States to prevent any unnecessary gaps of time. Every minute was important. The day after my Mom arrived we went to the doctor and I asked to speak to him before she went into the exam room. Mom was not happy that I did that, but I had to say something. I explained my concerns and observations of her not eating and not going to the bathroom regularly. I had also noticed many self-medicated laxatives in her medicine cabinet, which in my opinion said something was wrong in that area. As my Mom went into the exam room she told me she was not happy with me discussing her with the doctor without her. What could I say except okay Mom, I am sorry. I was sorry but I wanted the doctor to know everything I observed. I wanted him to be equipped with any information that could help determine the problem quickly. I wanted my Mom to be treated as soon as possible because I could not imagine my life without my Mom.

The doctor wanted a colonoscopy scheduled after the examination and the appointment was made for three weeks out. I was in shock!!! I called the specialist when I found out the scheduled colonoscopy date and stated my Mom will be dead in three weeks, that I need her to be seen sooner. They told me if someone cancelled they would call me. I kindly and respectfully stated I will call every ½ an hour to find out if anyone cancels. I called about 5 or 6 times that day, and then they FOUND an opening. Unfortunately the office had called my Mom at my home first and she fussed at them for talking to me about the appointment. OH MY GOODNESS!!! MOM!!! I am trying to help. On top of that I called the house phone and Tiffany had answered the phone, but I did not know my Mom also picked up as well. I asked Tiffany if Grandmom had eaten the fruit I left for her for breakfast and if she had gone to the bathroom. Well, Mom heard that and was upset once again. This was so unbelievable that she was fighting me with every step I took.

The amount of vacation and or personal days I had remaining at work were now scarce, and I had to restrict the amount of time I was now out of the office. The day of the appointment I asked Marvin to take my Mom to the doctor while I went to work and if there was anything serious to call me, and I would leave work. I had to work, I had a family to take care of including my mother, which takes money. The reality of working for an employer is they want you to work, they say they understand but it's really not sincere since the work has to get done. *(This is where my Uncle would in the future say I didn't care to take my Mom to the doctor and that Marvin had to take her.) This Uncle was such a fabricator. In my opinion he takes part of the truth, just enough of the truth and twists it to what sick perspective he needs to tell his tales…*

Unfortunately Marvin called me and the news was not good at all. I immediately left work, ran to my car and flew down the highway to the hospital where the colonoscopy procedure was completed, in the city. The doctors said my Mom had a serious blockage, and emergency surgery needed to be done. I made several phone calls to family and friends. The surgery was scheduled and so many of my Mom's friends from all over the world just called day and night for Sister Nelson.

I was finding this whole thing hard to comprehend as life as I knew it was so rapidly changing. I felt pressured on every angle, work was terrible… I hated my job, my church was falling apart with unhappy parishioners, I had issues at home and now my rock, my Mom was not in a good place. I was about to go into a deep abyss. I felt myself becoming numb, I had to somehow be strong. I had to take care of my girls.

Prior to my Mom's surgery I spoke to the doctors and the surgeon. The surgeon was a French man that had an amazing gift to save people's lives by successfully performing complicated surgeries. The physicians themselves could not believe my Mom was even alive. They had to operate to truly see what was going on inside of her but they knew from the colonoscopy test that there was a major blockage. Doctor after doctor came to examine my Mom, they asked did she have pain,

and asked question after question.

Chapter 7

On the day of surgery the surgeon came and spoke to me and explained the options, I listened intensely and thanked him for all he was doing to help my Mom. This was my Mommy, my Mom and to me no one could conceptualize what I was going through. Two of my Mom's friends from church where she pastored in Connecticut, stayed with me at the hospital the entire time of the surgery. My dad had his own other family but was constantly helping with how to handle the legal matters like paying the bills etc. I think I was in a daze while the surgery was going on, I just kept talking to God and asking what to do, how to do it, help her, heal her, save her. Finally after six hours the surgeon comes through the double doors and speaks with me. He said they will have to resection the intestines and she had a large tumor that must have been present for some time, since they cannot tell where it starts and stops. The tumor appears to have begun in the intestines and fused with her stomach and liver. She had to be given a colostomy. He said the purpose of the colostomy they were creating was for comfort, since at this point the removal of the tumor was not an option nor was there a true option of chemotherapy or radiation. What was I hearing? Mom has colon cancer stage 100. The next day my dad drove from Pittsburgh, his brother from New York and my aunts all on my dad's side came to visit Mom. The phone rang so much. I had to keep repeating myself, describing what was happening with mom, to our large family and circle of friends. I could not call everyone, I was drained, and my Mom was so challenging. As I reflect maybe she was angry with how her life had ended up. I have no idea.

At this point, my ex-husband was out and most forms of communications had stopped since I see life is "short" as they say and I could not take his lying, cheating and freeloading anymore. Now it was me and the girls, which financially made no difference since freeloaders do not really contribute. Ahhhh I digress.

After the surgery my Mom and I were shown how to treat, take care of and replace the colostomy bag. We had to decide where she would go after leaving the hospital as a terminally ill patient. Tiffany, my older daughter was not dealing with this situation well at all. How could I take care of my Mom at home with the girls? The living room would have to be transformed into a hospital room, and emotionally I truly did not know how to handle the situation. She needed care 24 hours of the day, she could not eat and she was almost skin and bones. Both of my mother's brothers came to the States and stayed by my home for at least a week each, independently to visit Mom. While we were in the hospital room one evening, I decided to bring up the situation about the status of her life and does she understand what the doctors are saying.

Prior to mentioning this to Mom, I had a deep prayer with God and asked how I should talk to my Mom about the situation. I was having a hard time understanding why this was happening to such a faithful Christian who spent her entire life preaching and teaching about God. I asked him to heal my mother and have her come out of this. I asked him to keep her in her right mind. I cried and cried and cried and then very clearly as if I am standing next to you I heard God say "my thoughts are not your thoughts, neither are your ways my ways…as the heavens are higher than the earth, so are my ways higher than your ways and my thoughts than your thoughts". Isaiah 55:8-9. I asked are you going to take her, and the answer was yes. God said he would strengthen me and not leave me, he said, in this world you will have trials and tribulations but be of good cheer, I have overcome the world. That was the end of the conversation, so I knew to some extent some of what was ahead of me. This would be one of the deepest valleys in my life.

I prayed for the right words to say to my Mom, I never told her about my prayer or the words I heard…. Back in the hospital room we continued to talk about what the doctors had said. Mom had three choices:

1. Move to my house
2. Move to a nursing home
3. Move to a hospice

At first, she stated she would like to move with me but did not think it would be best with me working and the kids seeing her the way she is day after day. I mentioned hospice and she became upset and said she her first preference was to stay with me and the second was a nursing home. The nursing home wanted $5000.00 a month and neither one of us could afford that bill. This is how the business of the healthcare industry is structured. The doctors and nurses typically want to take care of you, however the reality is, hospitals are a business and they require money. We talked about death that night, meeting God and what she wanted for her services. In general this is not an easy topic to discuss. I needed to find out what Medicare benefits covered for her and her insurance from the United Church. My mother's brother, Cornelius became very angry with me for bringing up death to my mother. I asked her about her wishes if something were to happen.

We even talked about what she wanted to wear and then Cornelius became infuriated. I also asked her what about the house in Grenada and she said finish it. I told her I would take care of her wishes and whatever she wanted. Her brother and I left the hospital shortly after that to return to my home, where he was staying while in town.

Once we arrived home, my Uncle quickly called his brother Jerome and little did I know that the plotting against me had begun. I was glad when he left since he was so picky with his food and wanted special food to eat. He couldn't eat this or that and I just did not have the energy nor desire to cook. I do not think I cooked for almost an entire year. Before Mom left the hospital, I had been speaking with my dad and my paternal Uncles on how to handle this overwhelming situation. I was so stressed. I tried to talk to the hospital about the billing and medical information. I tried to handle everything, but I quickly began to stumble because I needed a Power Of Attorney for the hospital to talk to be in detail about her situation, as well as the church that held her benefits information to see what was covered and with social security to see what Medicare covered also. I had to get a Power of Attorney. A friend of mine was a lawyer and assisted me with obtaining the document and my Uncle Kyle had assisted me with a notary sealing their signature on the document, outside of a restaurant on top of the hood of the car. The signatures were authentic, it's just that the notary was not on site at the time it was signed. When I took the papers to my Mom to sign, two pastors happened to be visiting my Mom, Reverend Griffith and another pastor who I can visualize as a short gray haired thin elderly man, but I just cannot remember his name. I asked for them to be witnesses. My mother was upset I had the paperwork and they told her that she should sign it and that I was only trying to help her and that I could have just abandoned her. I would have never abandoned her but that's what the man said. She called her brothers and they told her not to sign it until they had read it, as if I was going to do something to harm her. I have no idea what other poison they put in her head that day. By now, I began to believe her brothers were crazy and had ulterior motives. Why did they need to read it, why did they have to be involved? They were not making the calls to Social Security, or to the United Church benefits coordinator or handling her bills. My Mom finally signed the paper that day after quarrelling with me. What was the issue with her brothers? Did they want to come up to the States and deal with these agencies? She was my mother and I was going to help her anyway that I could. I eventually was able to find out what the medical insurance covered and how to deal with the payments. This is all I used to document for, otherwise I put the document away.

Chapter 8

From June to November, I visited my Mom every day after work, except for two days during that time frame. The girls and I would change our clothes from work and school and pack our things to visit my Mom. For the two days I missed during the six months, her brother Cornelius called and asked me, when last have you seen your Mom. I told him I see her every day except for those two days when I was just so tired. He stated he didn't believe me since my Mom told him she couldn't remember the last time she saw me. Imagine that, I just shook my head because every single day I would get home and take the girls to visit my Mom and we would eat dinner with her and do their homework, and this man who lived in another country got mad at me for missing two days. With regards to the decision for my Mom to go into hospice, I am at complete peace, especially when she told me that it was the best choice that could have been made. Every day I watched my Mom deteriorate more and more and begin to slip away. She was very strong and the nurses and doctors were amazed that she was still alive.

One afternoon, one of the hospital officials asked if they could meet with me and the doctor, on the upcoming Wednesday afternoon to talk about my Mom's condition. A day or two after I had agreed, Mom told me she had found out about the intended meeting and asked me how could I plan a meeting to discuss her without her being there. First of all, I had no idea what the doctors wanted to say to me and I just said yes to the meeting. The kicker is she told her brothers about this meeting and her brothers felt I was up to something. Up to what? What could I be up to with meeting the doctors? These individuals, my Uncles, had fully annoyed me to my last nerve. Wednesday rolled around and I left work early to attend the meeting. My Mom was rolled into the meeting room within the hospice unit. It was a small room with a sofa and a couple of lazy-boy chairs. My Mom started out by saying thank goodness I found out about this meeting. I just looked at my Mom and asked the doctors what was this meeting about? Apparently Medicare would no longer pay for her stay in hospice since Mom said she was not in pain and was doing fine. She said God was going to heal her and she was going to walk out of there. Well if we fast forward she was right. She did leave the hospice unit and went to Grenada but went down-hill quickly there without any medication and proper care. I must say that God does perform miracles all the time, and God is sovereign.

I asked the doctor, if my Mom stated she was in pain, then would everything be covered and they responded by saying yes. The thing is Mom was not in pain because the doctors and nurses gave her medication to take the pain away and she didn't know it and didn't believe it. They were trying to make sure she was comfortable and she refused to believe she was getting medication. My Mom was in such rare form, she sat up and said I am so glad I heard about this meeting, I am not in pain and I am not going to say I am in pain because I am not. She was rolled back to her room after the meeting and I just sat there for a minute and the hospice official gave me a hug and said I am so sorry. He said, I know she is being difficult and sometimes people lash out at the ones closest to them. I went back to my Mom's room and she told me she wanted me to take some money out of her account and send it to the church in Grenada as an offering. I remember telling my dad and Uncle Jake and my Uncle Jake told me to read a book about the various stages of dying and how to handle the death of a loved one. I read a couple of books, twice, and to this day the information I learned was unforgettable. The books helped me deal with the entire process tremendously, and discussed imminent death. In the various books, and articles, it mentions the multiple stages of death and one of them was bargaining. I am not saying my Mom was bargaining with God by asking me to send money to the church. I am just saying this was mentioned as a stage in the material I read, and I recognized it. I loved my Mom so much and could not understand how if she preached about seeing God for almost all of her life, that she did not want to believe he actually wanted her back home with him. She said she could not possibly die now because too many people were praying for her and there was so much work to do for God's kingdom. Maybe God just wanted her home and to do kingdom work in heaven.

The day after this meeting with the hospice staff, my mother's brother Cornelius called me, asking about what happened at the meeting. I told him what happened at the meeting and he appeared angry that the meeting was even scheduled. Here's the thing, the brothers of my mother at least 2 of them had never lived in the US and have no idea about Medicare and health care insurance processing and just thought I was trying to pull something fraudulent. They poisoned my ill mother with these thoughts. They told her to come to Grenada and they would take care of her and she would not have to go through all of what she is going through up there in the United States. They actually told her this. I could not believe. I told them she is definitely ill and the reality is Mommy is dying. She would tell them on the phone oh I can take care of myself down there, and they are not feeding me in the hospice and that she could take care of her own colostomy and so on. I just could not believe it.

I asked the doctors for a list of her medications and the list was two pages long. My dad even visited my Mom again to talk to her and she told him, "his days of giving her advice were over once they got divorced", so that was the end of that. Oh my God in heaven please help me I would cry out, because I do not know what else to do. I did not want my Mom to go to Grenada because, the Caribbean may be a beautiful place to visit, live and retire, but it is not a place to get sick and need major medical care.

Chapter 9

At this point when the kids and I would visit my Mom in hospice and she constantly talked about returning to Grenada. I would get so upset with her because Tiffany would have panic attacks from hearing her say this and have to be rushed to the hospital Emergency Room connected to the hospice building. I had to stop taking Tiffany so often and either go on my own or with Nina. One night my Mom called me and told me that her roommate had passed and that the body was still in the room and that she had to get out of that place because so many people are dying there. I talked to her for a while until she felt a little better. I called the nurses station to ask them when the roommate was going to be removed because it was not a good situation for my Mom to be in at this point or any point really.

No one could tell me how long she had to live, that was completely up to God but I knew it would happen because of my prayer discussions with God, and I was thankful that I was essentially able to say a long good bye and spend time with my Mom. I felt like I was in some sort of daze, since my Mom had always been there for me and with me. This situation really makes you think and be thankful for each day you have with your loved ones.

The day came for me to actually take my Mom back to Grenada. I booked the plane tickets for me and my Mom to take her to Grenada, her place of birth. I think if she had told me she wanted to die in Grenada and be buried there I would have been more receptive to her desire, but that's not what she said. She said she was going there and could get proper food to eat there that would make her stronger and get better. In an act of desperation I called her brother Jerome. I tried to explain to him the list of medications that she is taking and asked if he could check to see if those medications were available on the island. I also called my aunt Megan, his wife to tell her that he and my mother had planned on her staying there with them until my Mom was strong enough to go back to her home herself. I explained the colostomy, which I was very nervous about, and needed to make sure she did not get an infection. There was a list of over 20 medications that my Mom was taking and she told her brother it was not true. This man wanted control of my mother for whatever reason and was feeding her nonsense that she was not as sick as the doctors were telling her. I faxed the list of medications to him at that time and then called to make sure he received it. He said that of course all of this medication was available on island. I asked him if someone there knew how to take care of a person who had a colostomy. He said of course my wife is a nurse she will know what to do. My dad called him two days before we were to leave to speak with him and he hung up on my dad. My Mom really needed care, she could not be on her own and for whatever reason her crazy brothers were not getting that idea in their head. I had to take her to Grenada, you may wonder why I did, but that is what she wanted. As much as it pained me in my soul for her to leave the States, I had to fulfill her wishes. I remember the nurse saying to me, your mother thinks and is expecting God to personally come down here and perform some miracle, this is going to be a hard lesson for her and it's not going to happen like that. I never responded. What was I to say? My Mom really had a right to believe whatever she wanted to believe and if she thought God was going to heal her, then who am I to say otherwise. All things are possible.

To prepare for the trip I purchased boost, wound care stuff, colostomy bags and filled prescriptions for all of her medications, but could only get enough for 30 days. I didn't even know if the airline would allow her to actually board the plane. The morning of the flight, I got to the hospice unit of the hospital very early. The nurse told me she would have her dressed, however once I got there she was not dressed and of course she could not dress herself. I fussed when I arrived and the nurse for that day just didn't care. She thought it was madness for my Mom to be going to Grenada. We got to the airport and the line was incredibly long. I had my Mom sit down in a wheelchair to the side with a friend of hers that came to see her off.

At that time the airport in Grenada did not have a ramp to just walk off of the plane. You had to walk down the stairs to exit the plane. I had asked the airline about her exiting and they said it would have to be scheduled from the Grenada side. I asked my Uncle Jerome ahead of time to schedule the lift to help her off the plane, and he said okay. Wouldn't you know it… he had not because in all of his brightness he believed that I was over exaggerating my Mom's condition and when we arrived nothing was scheduled. I told the stewardess that she cannot walk down the steps, as a matter of fact she fell down onto one knee when she was getting on the plane. It was a miracle that they didn't say anything, but they kept looking at her the entire flight. When we landed in Grenada my Mom said thank you Jesus and tears fell from her eyes. I was glad she did not have to go to the bathroom because I just would not know how I could fully assist on the plane in the plane's bathroom. Back to getting off the plane, nothing was scheduled so the airport staff brought some sort of high back chair with back wheels, strapped her in and manually lifted her down the stairs. We came out of the terminal and then to add insult to injury my Uncle was late. My mother's District Superintendent from the Walton church was at the airport and actually asked me if this was my Mom. I answered yes, and yes, she had looked that different. A whole half an hour later the brother and his son arrived at the airport and said they got the time mixed up, imagine that. Owen, my cousin asked why did my Mom look like that and her brother said oh it must be the long flight that took a lot out of her. I let her go with her brother and I went to rent a vehicle to then meet them at the house. Later my Uncle Jerome would say in a typed letter to me that I abandoned my mother when we got to Grenada. So if you were not at the airport and you did not know I went to rent a vehicle and then meet them at the house you would not know what I did, except I got to the house a little later than when they got to the house. I had to wait in line to get the car, fill out papers and then drive the car to the house which was 40 minutes away from the airport in which my Uncle had a 35 minute head start or even longer. At that time the relationship was bruised but not severed as yet. It was as if I was constantly explaining myself with these wicked people.

I stayed with my Mom for a few days and tried my best to organize everything I thought she would need.

Her brother Cornelius put up balloons saying get well soon. The brothers were so cold to me. I asked my Mom why are her brothers doing this and told her I am trying my best to make sure she was okay. I had to say goodbye to my Mom and that was just so difficult. My Uncle Jerome had asked me to leave my mother's check book with him. He became irate when I did not leave it and began to slam doors and drawers looking for it in the house.

Chapter 10

I returned to Grenada a few weeks later to visit my Mom. She told me when I was coming to bring the strong medication. I told her I left all of the medication there. I had packed clothes for a funeral for my visit. I somehow knew this would be the last time I would be seeing my Mom alive. A few weeks before, when I was at my Mom's house visiting, my Uncle Jerome insisted he was in charge. He went and got a Power of Attorney and told her he needed that document to take care of her. He only wanted one since I had Power of Attorney in the States, but that was to allow me to talk to Medicare and handle the medical and banking on behalf of my Mom. This was so un-believable. He wanted me to leave him her money and check book and I refused. I wanted to know what bills needed to be paid and told him I would pay them. He told people I would not allow my Mom to stay at home with me and that I did not care anything about her. I know this because when I was visiting my Mom in Grenada, one of the ladies hired by my Uncle Jerome to help out my Mom told me that is what my Uncle told her and she realized this was not true and she wanted no parts of this situation. I could not believe it, I just could not. My world just kept getting darker and darker. I was in the middle of a divorce, I had two young daughters and I was trying to figure out how to take care of my Mom in this terminal situation from the States.

I prayed with the caretaker and told God that I needed help right away. I needed to leave the island and I wanted to know if I should leave the check book or not and I needed a clear answer. Right after I finished praying there was a knock on the door. I went to the door to see who was there. It was Reverend Kenton, a good friend of my Mom and our family. He asked me how I was doing and I immediately told him about my Uncle wanting me to leave the check book. He sat down and said to me, do not leave this check book with this man. This man is not honest, take the check book with you home. That was my answer from God. Take the check book and that is what I did. I had been given the strength and direction I needed. Reverend Kenton prayed with me and then left. He was always such a nice man and pastor.

I also realized when my Uncle brought food for my Mom he would buy chicken back and ask the caretakers to make something out of that for her. I just cried and cried. How could I do my part from the States, why did she leave the States? God why is this happening? Chicken back? What is that nonsense? I felt as if he didn't care anything about her. While on this last trip to Grenada, Uncle Jerome had vigils by her bedside and would try and physically block me from getting near her while she was in the bed. Finally I just got in the bed with her and laid next to her while he was there singing to her. He got mad at the fact I was in the bed with her and he soon ended his visit and left the house. You could feel his anger. At some point my Uncle Jerome said to me, your mother wants you to leave the house. I said what, what do you mean? I said Mom you want me to leave and she said yes. At this point I just did not know what to think. He was just sitting there smiling. I packed up my girls and we went to a hotel not too far from the house but I was at the house constantly except to sleep there. I think she was afraid of him at this point.

The morning of the 3rd of December I got a call from the caretaker that my Mom was dying and that she could hear the death rattle. I jumped up and got the girls up, told them I would be right back and I drove up the hill full speed. As I was driving I got another call that she had passed. It could not have been 15 minutes since I received the phone call. As I pulled into the driveway I saw my Uncle Jerome and a cousin of mine, which told me that they were called long before me and arrived before me. I waked around them and went straight into my Mom's room. My Uncle Jerome followed me into the bedroom where my mother was, for whatever reason. I just cried and cried. Owen, a cousin of mine went to get the girls for me from the hotel. I did not want them to see what had happened. My Uncle Jerome listened as I told my cousin where the girls were located. When the girls reached the house I had them stay out in the living room. I know they wanted to know what was going on with Grandmom and I had to tell them that she was gone. My other cousin called the funeral director and I sat on the sofa with the girls. My Uncle Jerome said someone needed to stay at the house and my aunt, his wife told him that I would be staying there at my Mom's place. The look he gave me was horrible. The lay leader of the church my mother pastored came to the house and told me I could stay at the house for as long as I needed to. I stayed and watched the funeral director wrap up my Mom in the body bag and place her in the hearse. That was a sight that I cannot get out of my mind. I left the house and went to the hotel, packed up our things and went back to my Mom's house.

I remembered my conversation with my Mom when I asked her about a will. I remembered her telling me that she did not have one nor did she need one since I was her only child and that she was not married. I remember telling her that her brothers were treating me badly and asking her if she knew why. At some point on one of my trips, she asked me to dial Uncle Jerome's number and I did. She then told him I was not happy with what was happening, which I'm sure made him more irate. I believe at that point she had started to realize he was a terror but it was too late for her to do anything.

The caretaker told me that she talked to my Mom and my Mom said my Mom never wanted me to leave the house. This made me feel better and let me know my Mom loved me. Her brother said those words and not her. It was as if she was afraid to say something since I would not be there on island the entire time and that he would be there. I am so sorry she had to deal with this nonsense during her last days.

The very night my Mom died, my Uncle Jerome called me at her house and told me not to do anything with her things at the house since he was in charge of her house. He was acting like he was some sort of dictator over me. I said what are you talking about. He said he would be the one to distribute her things. I told him he lost his mind and that I don't care what he says. I started packing some of the things that night. I was selecting who would get certain items like clothing. I just could not believe I had to deal with these things so soon, but I knew I had to return home within a short period of time. I called the head of the church the next day and they told me I was fine to stay there and to not give my Uncle

Jerome the keys. They said he was not in charge of the mansion house for their church. For this very reason he made sure to not include any of her church members on the program of her funeral.

This was a pastor and I just was so confused as to what was happening. Why did God allow this craziness to happen? I felt as if my world was and had drastically changed. From that moment, my life was labeled, "before my Mom died" and after my Mom died". I was not able to trust people and kept people at an arm's length. This was my way of protecting myself since I learned, not all smiles are true smiles and not all people that laugh and hang out with you really care for you. My reaction may be drastic but what was I to think when family members that I grew up with, visited each other's houses and vacationed together, has such a secret hatred for me. These issues were all on my maternal side of the family. My paternal side of the family were great but they were in the States and I was in Grenada alone with the girls.

As the next few days went by, I tried to contact my mother's brothers to find out what was happening and what were the plans for the service. My Mom knew a lot of people and a lot of people knew her. People were calling from all over the world and people were stopping by the house asking me when was the service, who was on the program, what hymns were going to be sang. I had no answers. I had to call the superintendent of the church to complain and only then did my Uncle Jerome contact me to discuss the service. He came to the house with the superintendent and we discussed the service. I said I did not want her buried at the cemetery in town, I wanted her buried in Lamont. The cemetery in town was horrific and not well tended. Occasionally people would see bones and pieces of coffins and I did not want that for my Mom. My Uncle Cornelius said she will be buried in town, since he thought Lamont was too far for people to drive out there. I prayed and asked God to intercede, I did not want her there in town. As the days passed I was told that the cemetery in town was closed temporarily, which meant my Mom had to be buried in Lamont. Thank you God for granting me this request, I was so relieved.

The next day my Uncle Jerome called me at the house and said for me to meet him at the funeral home to view my mother's body and select a casket. My three Uncles stated they wanted to split the cost of my Mom's funeral between all of us. When we met at the funeral home, I was so shocked to see the way my Mom looked. She was still wrapped in the bed sheet and she actually had an icicle hanging from one of her teeth. Oh Mommy I thought. It did not have to be like this. I was in this other country where I used to only know happiness and now I have no control or say as to what is happening with her death. I was just a complete mess. I called my dad to ask for advice in what to do next and he would talk to me but I guess he struggled with how much to help because of extenuating circumstances. I felt truly alone. Thank goodness for my dear friend Amanda and Tony as well.

My Uncle told me as we were leaving the funeral home that we were not having a repass at all. What could I say? The funeral was set for the 11th of December. One day before my second cousin Lonnie and his wife's return to the island from the States. Lonnie and wife were both nurses and had been very helpful in the medical care of my Mom. They cleaned the opening of her colonoscopy bag when she was alive. Replacement colonoscopy bags were not even on island. Lonnie and his wife Claudia were familiar with caring for this type of situation since they were nurses in the States for over 30 years, and had retired in Grenada. Lonnie would tell me that my Mom would call him and ask him to help her with changing and cleaning the bag. This just pained me because she left the States where she was receiving good care. My Uncles had convinced her she could get better care in Grenada, which was complete madness. My mother's brothers were both upset that I did not agree to have her stay in my home. How could she stay in the house with me? I had to work and she needed full time care and I didn't want my girls to be subjected to the situation at home. My Godmother came from St Vincent and stayed with me 6 weeks to help me out during this time. Every day after work I would get the kids and we would eat dinner at the hospice unit. The only reason I remained sane was because God kept me from going insane. The ONLY reason.

Now Mom is gone and my world is completely upside down and inside out. I had an overwhelming sense of being alone in the world, and the battle was only beginning. The night before the funeral I had no idea how I was getting to the funeral. I could not believe I had to drive myself and my girls. The morning of the funeral I received a call from my Uncle Cornelius asking if I needed a ride. Can you believe it, it was if I was an afterthought or some sort of outsider. It was as if my

Uncles were saying…Oh that girl that is for my sister needs a ride is what it felt like.

The family met at the funeral home prior to the church service. I provided the outfit for my Mom and I thought she looked beautiful. It was the lavender dress we previously spoke about and her matching church hat. She never went into church without a church hat and I wanted to honor that for her final service.

The funeral director spoke to me and told me whatever I wanted to happen would happen and my Uncle Jerome was not happy he said that to me. Why did this man hate me so much? You could feel the hatred in in the room, I just could not figure it out at that time.

At the church the custom I was told was for the coffin to be at the back of the church and people viewed the body in the back. I went and sat in the front and the funeral director told me he would come and get me to do the final closing of the casket. When he came and got me I positioned myself and my girls in such a way that it was our private moment. I did not turn around to include my Uncles. Why should I, this was my mother. In the past days all he kept telling people was "this was my sister" as if he ranked higher than me. This would be the case as we will later find out he actually thought he came before me in the natural order of life. Do not ignore your senses or that little voice warning or guiding your steps.

When the girls and I went to Grenada to see about my Mom before she passed I knew we were going to be going to her funeral. I had bought and packed our clothes for the funeral. I knew it because I prayed and God told me again, he said my ways are not your ways and my thoughts are higher than your thoughts. I knew he gave me a chance to say goodbye. I was able to read a poem at her funeral and could not believe my Uncle Cornelius actually asked me for a copy of the poem, which "I never got around to doing that".

After the service, the girls and I got a ride to the cemetery from my Uncle Cornelius. Songs were sang at the gravesite. I moved the flowers I bought for Mom from me and the girls to the head of Mom's grave. My Uncle Jerome did not like that and had his flowers moved to the head of her grave and moved mine over. I just did not have the fight in me to do anything else at that time. My Aunt Megan then came over to me at the grave site and said "we are having something over at the house, you and the girls are welcomed to come". I was in shock. They planned a repass and at the gravesite I was being told I was invited. I told my Aunt Megan, no thank you and that I would never cross the threshold to their house ever again. My Aunt Megan is really a nice person. Only my Aunt Megan told me about the repass. She was trying to just be her nice self as she has always been to me and my girls.

I got my ride home, walked into Mom's house, and the girls and I sat on the sofa in the dark alone for hours. We just say there staring at the wall.

My friend Amanda and Tony later came over and sat with me and Tony bought me and the girl's food. A few hours later, my Godmother, Cousin Cheryl, Cousin Nakita and Aunt Megan came by the house and sat with us for a bit. I went into my Mom's room and packed some of my Mother's church hats and gave them to Hyacinth, my Godmother. It was an awkward time but I had to leave to go back to the States by the end of the following week and she was leaving to go back to St Vincent the next morning.

That night I sat up and starred at my Mom's room and watched my girls sleep. Tiffany was so close with her Grandmom. They called each other every day and this deeply affected her. Nina was still young but would miss her Grandmom immensely as well.

Chapter 11

The next morning, I received a call from my Uncle Jerome telling me that he was in charge of the Mansion house and that I was to not touch anything, not even my Mom's clothes and that he would decide everything since he had Power of Attorney. He found out that I gave my Godmother some of my Mother's hats and was mad he was not part of the decision. I told him that Power of Attorney died when she took her last breath and that I would do as I pleased. He said he had me on tape and I said who cares, I'll repeat what I just said. I immediately started working to pack up the entire house. I gave her really nice clothes to her friends that I believed she would have wanted them to have certain items, and the rest I packed up and took to the Salvation Army. With regards to the living room furniture and washing machine, I was able to store it at my friends Tony's shipping container. The bedroom furniture which was really nice, I was able to move it to the bedroom in the apartment at Belmont. When the furniture was delivered to Belmont all the lights in the village went out just like the night when my Mom passed and we were turning over her mattress. From the time the bedroom set went in the house the lights went out for a few hours.

I packed and packed non-stop for days. I lost almost 20 pounds in two weeks. I only stopped packing to feed the girls. I could not sleep well and I could not eat. I went through every drawer and box etc. in the house. When I was ready to leave, the house was completely empty. I gave the keys to the church leaders and they expressed their sincere condolences and sadness for what had happened with my Uncles. Unfortunately this was not my Uncle Jerome's first time trying to take over at someone else's life. I took one last look at the house and then left for the airport. I thought that was the end of that chapter somewhat. I knew in the back of my head that at some point I would have to talk to my Uncle Cornelius about the land and the house up at Belmont, but now was not the time.

Chapter 12

Back home in the States I was trying to regain some type of normalcy. I was finally divorced, thank goodness. That was a unity that should have never happened, but I was young and very stupid and tried for years to get out of the situation and it was officially over a few weeks before my mother passed.

In February of 2004, while at home, there was a knock on the door. Tiffany said, Mom there's somebody at the door. I went to the door and said yes, how may I help you. It was a courier for a lawyer on behalf of my Uncle Jerome. I was so shocked. Two months after my mother passed, I received a hand delivered letter saying my Uncle Jerome was suing me for a chair that was my mothers. He was clearly upset that I had cleared out the house.

The letter read:

"Dear Mrs. Nelson:

Re: Your Uncle – Mr. Jerome Joseph

We are the Attorneys- At-Law for our above-named client.

We are instructed that you have knowingly taken into your possession a reclining chair which belongs to our client when you came to Grenada recently to attend your late mother's funeral.

Your Uncle Cornelius Joseph, and our client were sole contributors to your mother's welfare, financial and otherwise while she was alive, and he paid CBD $6,000.00 costs for her funeral, and our client paid the amount of CBD $3,500.00 for the cost of care for your late mother during her illness, while you contributed nothing.

You well knew the chair belongs to our client, but your knowledge notwithstanding, you add insult to your ingratitude by seeking to possess our client's property.

We put you on notice that unless you take the steps necessary to immediately return our client's chair to him, we will commence legal proceedings against you to recover not only the chair but also the amounts expended by our client and his brother.

Govern yourself accordingly,

Yours truly,

ATTORNEYS-AT-LAW

cc Jerome Joseph"

I could not believe the man was suing me for the chair my mother gave him money to go to the store and buy for her to be comfortable. He actually paid a lawyer to sue me for the chair that was in her house. I was beside myself, I just fell to the floor. How much more was I to take? This seemed to me like a nightmare that would not end.

I did not know if I should contact a lawyer in the United States or in Grenada. I decided to ignore that letter at that time, however I eventually selected a lawyer in Grenada to deal with the land situation. I also contacted the superintendent of the church my Uncle pastored, and sent him a copy of the letter from the lawyer. The church did not know what to do about him at that time, and decided to do nothing, at least to my knowledge. Many years later my Uncle began to harass that same Superintendent and tried to ruin his pastoral legacy. Life is interesting. Now the Superintendent was complaining about how ruthless my Uncle Jerome was to him. Interesting how life happens.

About a month later in March, I received another letter from my Uncle Jerome directly.

"Hello Sandra,

I am aware you are my niece and Rev. Eudalyn Nelson was your Mother, but she was also the sister of your Uncle Cornelius and myself…….

You have obviously become quite greedy in grabbing after all available funds to complete your dream house……..You brought your mother, Rev. Eudalyn Nelson to Grenada, and abandoned her. Please remember that you did not even accompany her home to Black Rock. It was your Uncle Cornelius, Nephew Owen, Rev. Peter Barnes and myself." (What madness since I went to get a rent a car and he took her home instead of her waiting on me). "I paid Crown House Furnishings $507.00 to complete the payment for the household items which you took from the Manse…… I spent $5705.62 CBD (documented) to take care of you mother from November 1 to the day of her passing all from my personal resources, including the Reclining Chair from Courts….. I do not expect to recover the above sums expended on my sister, Rev. Eudalyn Nelson, who is also your mother, but I have the legal rights to do so. If therefore you do not return the chair, it leaves me with no other choice. I will take whatever action necessary to recover that items, and all others since you are the beneficiary of significant sums which you are making arrangements to receive as a result of your Mother's passing……You have said that you have been advised that the Power of Attorney has no legal status now, and further that there is nothing I can do to recover the reclining chair. Let me trust that you will let good sense prevail, since I will recover it at any cost. I know where the items are stored, and could have legally recovered it already, but not without embarrassment.

I'm sure you will think again now.

Your Uncle."

This was so unbelievable. I cried for a while and then I called my friend Amanda and we were both in such shock. We then realized that this letter was from him directly and not the lawyer. There was nothing he could do legally. This was my mother and morally and legally I come before him. He was mad that I had not responded to the first letter from the lawyer. I did not react the way he anticipated and he had not thought his plan all the way through. We were now at a state where the relationship had severed. There was no turning back. This was horrific and egregious.

To me part of his hatred towards me stemmed from the house being built and the closeness that I had with my Mom. I had no regrets with my Mom except that she would not live to see the completion of the dream and her grandchildren grow up. I did everything I could have possibly done for her out of love. We told each other I love you always and hugged always.

Towards the end of my Mom's life we strongly disagreed with each other for her to return to Grenada. She died begging God to take her out of her pain. She begged God to call her name. The island did not have strong enough medication to take away the pain and there was nothing I could do. At one point I considered going to the streets to look and buy some medication for her but it never came to that. In Grenada, when mom was alive, I called the village nurse to come to the house with the doctor, the only blood pressure machine available was broken. The doctor said to me your mother is terminal and we do not have medication here to treat her. I showed him the list of medications I had received from the hospital/hospice doctors. The Doctor looked at the list and said none of these items are here on island. See if you are able to get some more.

This was my fear come true and why I tried so hard for her to stay in the States. The doctor said to me, "now there's nothing anyone here can do. It's all in Gods hand as to how much she suffers in pain and for how long". For two days my mother said "Spirit of the Living God, call my name in Jesus name". She was pleading for God to call her name to her eternal home. This was so painful to hear but taught me many lessons even at the time of her death. None of her "caretakers" knew how to handle this sickness. One of the things it taught me is that up until the end, my mother believed in our Heavenly Father and she held on to that to the end. Second it taught me that only what is done for Christ will last and that is all that matters. It also taught me that we have our plans for our life and that may not always line up with what are the plans and timing God has for our lives.

Before Mom passed she said to me finish the house. I am passing the baton on to you to finish. This would be part of the driving force I had behind me to finish the project no matter what. I remember Joseph in the bible telling his brothers of his dreams and I remember sermons saying be careful of who you tell your dreams. Not everyone will be happy for you. Sometimes they will go to great lengths to stop you from achieving your dream for whatever reason. Maybe they are just plain not happy with themselves or their own lives. I reflected on Nehemiah in the bible, with a sword in one hand and a tool in the other to continue building the wall. This would be one of the bible stories that encouraged me as I began the journey to finish this dream house. It was not just a house it was a means to fund the deep desire to do mentoring ministry around the world. I wanted to help others and make positive impacts into their lives. I wanted to be a blessing to somebody.

Chapter 13

When my mother was alive we would calculate the number of blocks and concrete needed for the various phases of the building project. In the beginning I was able to pay installments on the 8 inch and 6 inch concrete blocks. I was also able to put down 40% of the money for the concrete and pay the balance in installments. Each month I would faithfully make a payment. At that time my only choice was to mail checks. I called so much to the various companies that they knew me by my voice. I was intensely engaged in the project. My Mom was able to see the apartment almost built. She knew the windows had been installed and we had both walked on the concrete floor of the main house. The concrete floor of the main house was the roof of the apartment. Remember the second apartment actually happened by "mistake". An apartment in the front of the house was always the plan but now we were able to have at least two apartments.

Each phase of the house proved to have their own miracles. I would receive favor with sales on materials on the island and in the States. I would purchase materials in the states each pay and store them until I had enough material and money to either ship a barrel or a large box. I was able to establish relationships that allowed me to create a network to ship items, clear items in customs and transport them to the Belmont property or store at a friends until it was needed. I took the house as far as I could, but I stopped when my Mom died. 18 months after my Mom passed I contacted my Uncle Cornelius in Saint Croix. I asked him about the land and if he was going to still transfer the land. He told me he had no intentions of signing over the land and that he would make sure I never got the land and that the house would be his.

    All I could think about is, did I hear wrong. I began to question myself and if I truly heard God speaking to me about that dream and the completion of it and its purpose. I thought I should have just bought my free and clear piece of land like I originally wanted to do, but my Mom insisted that she was given this particular piece of land and why get something else. She said let's use what is already there. I funded the project but it was to be where my Mom could live during her retirement and we were to make money for her to travel the world as she chose and have a great income for me and the girls as well. What went wrong I kept thinking? Maybe I should just give up. I just had this feeling deep inside of me that would not go away, to not give up. Never give up.

For the next five years I did nothing with regards to the land nor the house. I would go to Grenada regularly and just go up to Belmont and look at it, and walk around it, trying to image what to do and how to do it. I had started dating again and just got caught up in life.

At age 40, in 2008 and 5 years after my Mom passed, I decided that I needed to contact a lawyer. I hired a lawyer in Grenada and explained the situation. The lawyer explained this would be a long process. What I had going for me was the document that was signed by my Uncle Cornelius, my mother and I. I was listed as a party to the handling of the construction and overseeing everything on behalf of my mother. I secured this document since 1999 not knowing that I would need this key record years later.

As the case proceeded, an affidavit was completed by my Uncle Cornelius and I had to complete one as well. Although these details are painful for me to hear again it is also reconfirmation that God is able to deliver us from our deepest valleys. This was a deep and dark valley for me. I never knew what it was like to have enemies that would lie about you and spew such venom about a person for whatever reason. One of the most hurtful lies was seeing my Uncle Cornelius actually write that I did not love my Mom and that I did not care about her. I tried my best to have her stay in the States where I knew she would at least not die in pain. This unfortunately did not happen. Her brothers talked her into returning to

Grenada where they could control everything and away from me her only daughter, and she died in terrible pain.

The amount of hatred these Uncles had towards me was thick. If it were not for God I would have lost my mind. I did not lose my mind and I am now able to share and tell others that no matter what has happened and is happening they can hold on to God and get through it. They can more than get through it. They can overcome it tremendously. They will smile again, and be at peace again and be much stronger and resilient.

Chapter 14

Included in the Affidavit my Uncle Cornelius stated:

"Throughout our discussion about our plans, it was clearly understood between my sister and me that the house to be built was for her sole benefit and not that of the Claimant. At no time, did I agree or contemplate the magnitude of the construction that is presently on the land. The size of the structure being built makes it appear that Sandra had the intention of using her mother's land for her own personal benefit. That was never my intention nor was it her mother's even though there was some discussion about renting out a part of the land to generate income for her, my sister. I never agreed to what appears to be a guest house of some sort to be built for the Claimant's enrichment. The land was being given to my sister for her own benefit and her retirement."

"At some point in time, my sister discussed my offer with her daughter, the Claimant. Her daughter telephoned me and asked me for permission to start the construction of a house for her mother. I gave it."

"Although Sandra informed me about the construction after it started, I did not see the building plans and did not know what she was building. I felt confident at the time that she would have built as agreed. When I first saw the building foundation, I was amazed at the size of the building. I wondered at Sandra's motive. I immediately spoke with my sister and she too was surprised at the size of the foundation building. It was larger than either of us had contemplated."

"The discussions between my sister and me never included the construction of such a large two-story dwelling. At most, it would have been a 2 or three bedroom single story dwelling house".

Based on the affidavit from my Uncle Cornelius, it appeared to me as if part of the problem was the size of the home and that he may have never really wanted to give my Mom the land. If you give someone something then whatever they chose to do with it is whatever they chose to do with it. The size of the home was an issue for him.

One evening I received a call from Marvin and he called to tell me that he was on a conference call with my Uncle Jerome and my Uncle Cornelius earlier in the day. He said both of my Uncles wanted to see if he would be willing to be an overseer of the land in trust for my girls. He said he recorded the conversation and even the part where my Uncles said they needed to find a way to bring me down. Unbelievable and even more unbelievable that Marvin recorded it and let me hear it. I asked him to forward the message to my home phone. I then called my dad and asked if he knew of a way that I could record the message on the answering machine to a cassette. My dad was the best for these types of situations. I went to the electronic store and got what my dad told me to get and went back home and was able to record it onto the tape. The next day I called my cousin Owen, my Uncle Jerome's son and played it for him over the phone. He said he was going to speak to his dad. He eventually spoke to his dad who said, he was a big man and could do whatever he wanted to do. Imagine the pastor, Uncle Jerome, on tape planning to harm his niece and bring her down. I sent a copy of the tape to my lawyer and I also let her hear it over the phone.

Marvin also asked me for the blueprints of the house. Ha, ha, ha. Why would I give him the blue prints I asked? He said he wanted to build a similar house and since blue prints cost so much, that perhaps I could give him a copy of the one's I have. Now I knew that was a lie. I knew my Uncles wanted the blue prints and Marvin probably thought if he gave me some information I would maybe give him the blue prints. My speculation is they thought they would win the house in court and then need the blue prints to move forward. Very sad.

I believe one of the thoughts both of my Uncles had was to frustrate me and bring me to exhaustion to give up on the house. However, I had an inner strength that had been given to me and as far as I was concerned this battle was much bigger than me. This was a major spiritual battle taking place, in which I was being given strength to endure. I could not have done any of this on my own. I had to fly back and forth to Grenada numerous times and courier back and forth originally signed court documents. At one point in time I actually paid someone's ticket to fly from Grenada to Saint Croix to deliver papers from the court to my Uncle Cornelius to sign to keep the traction of the process.

All building on the house had stopped since I did not know how the court would rule. The consideration was to either re-pay me for the value of the property or award me the property. I did not want the funds, I wanted to continue what my mother and I started. My Uncle Cornelius asked for receipts for the house since he did not agree with the valuation that was provided to the court.

Chapter 15

Kevin and I flew down to Grenada for the court case. I organized all associated documents and supporting documents in a large binder. The 4 inch binder had a table of contents page and was sectioned with tabs to help me locate any documents I may need to show the Judge very quickly. All documents were also incased in full clear page protectors. When we entered the court room early in the morning I immediately recognized my Uncle Cornelius sitting in one of the chairs. We just sat in the waiting room for about two hours wondering what was happening in the court room. Finally we were called in and I had to enter the Judge's chamber alone with my Uncle Cornelius and our lawyers as well as the Judge. My Uncle Cornelius opened his briefcase with and pulled out some sort of CD that had my name on it. The

Judge did not want to hear or see the cd and to this day I have no idea what was on the cd.

The Judge asked me "what is that large binder" and I answered all of my supporting documents for the case in chronological order, your honor. She then asked me to pass her my binder. She flipped through the binder and then placed both of her arms on top of the binder and then began a mediation discussion. One of the things my Uncle Cornelius mentioned to the Judge, was how upset he was that I obtained power of attorney in the States for my Mom. The Judge asked me if I had the document and I said yes your honor it is in the book. She gave me the book and I opened the book at gave her the Power of Attorney document. She reviewed the document and told my Uncle Cornelius it appears to be a typical American Power of Attorney. He said he thought it was too sweeping and gave me too much power. My Uncle Cornelius thought he should have been the one or one of the individuals that was in charge of my Mom's affairs. The Judge stated, the person who created and organized this book of documents, does not appear to need any assistance in handling her mother's affairs.

The Judge asked;

1. Did Sandra do anything illegal with the Power of Attorney
   - Response - no
2. Did Sandra do anything immoral with the Power of Attorney
   - Response - no
3. Did Sandra take advantage of having the Power of Attorney
4. * Response – no

Sandra

1. Why did you need the Power of Attorney

    - Response – I needed this to talk to the hospital about my mother's condition.
    - I needed this document to talk to Medicare (medical insurance) about her medical coverage for treatment
    - I needed to talk to her creditors to pay her bills and ask about balances due.
    - I needed to talk to her medical insurance provider to about medical coverage limits
    - I needed to talk to her medical insurance provider about pharmaceutical coverages

Mr. Joseph this seems reasonable, said the Judge. It does not appear as if she has done any wrong. My Uncle Cornelius began to cry. He then said this was not supposed to go like this. The Judge began to ask questions about the location of the land and the monies spent. Uncle Cornelius said he did not believe the amount of money claimed to be spent on the existing dwelling. My lawyer stated, the building is there. It is a concrete structure up to ring beam. With an apartment underneath of the property. The survey document of the land was reviewed, however two of the parcels of the land were equal in size and my Uncle tried to tell the court that the parcel that did not have the house on the land was the parcel that had the house on it. I disagreed with his statement and insisted I knew exactly which parcel was the correct one. The Judge signed the order for the land to be reviewed and the right parcel with the building be signed over. (My Mom had asked for some additional land in front of the land where the house was located, to accommodate a pool towards the sea and my Uncle had agreed. Since we had not started that part of the project I did not feel it was appropriate to argue over that point and I let it go. It would have been nice and I would have loved to have it added unto the home. I always felt a sort of peace whenever I walked on the land.)

The ruling was made, and what a relief. Kevin and I left the court room and prayed. I was so thankful that this phase of the battle was completed.

I had to arrange to have the survey department representative verify the correct parcel of land on which the building stood. This took a couple of weeks and the document given to my lawyer by the survey department showed my Uncle Cornelius had indeed stated the wrong parcel of land in court. I will never know if this was done on purpose or not, and actually it is irrelevant since the correct parcel was identified by the survey department.

Chapter 16

I thought everything was moving along nicely at this point. It has now been seven years since my mother passed. I received a call from my lawyer that the court agreed to separate the land and have the ½ acre placed into my name. However…. Oh my goodness…..I could not believe I was hearing a however. My Uncle did not pay taxes on his land for over 10 years and before the court will divide the land the taxes will need to be paid.

Well, a letter was sent to my Uncle Cornelius in St. Croix stating the situation and I guess he was just laughing to himself at this point, since he was not going to pay the taxes. Can you believe this I said to myself, really God? I had already paid tens of thousands for the lawyer fees and the executive administrative fees.

I did not have money for ten years' worth of taxes. I asked if it mattered who paid for the taxes. Basically the court could care less who paid the taxes just as long as the taxes were paid. Only then would the land be able to be separated. I was just numb. I saved for two and half years and paid off the taxes on the land.

During that ten year span, I had re-married, moved into a brand new house as a blended family in another state, went back to school and obtained my Bachelor of Science degree in Business, and got a better job making significantly more money. While all of the darkness was going on with the property in Grenada God was blessing me in so many other areas of my life. I was working as a consultant in Houston, Texas and I loved the job. The consulting job in Houston gave me a huge salary increase and allowed me to save for the taxes owed on the land in Grenada. I also got to attend Riverview church every Wednesday evening for the time I was in Houston, 2 ½ years.

As a side note and shout out to God, many years maybe eight to ten years before getting the consulting job in Texas I remember listening to a sermon by James Bishop. I prayed to God and asked if it were possible, I would like to go to this church at least once to see it and hear a message. I remember looking it up to see where the church was located and then saying to myself oh my…I'm not sure how I would get there. Oh God if at all possible I would like to not to have to pay for the trip to Houston, Texas. I laughed to myself since I wondered how would that be possible but I asked anyway. Fast forward I was working in Houston and staying at a long term residence hotel during the week, Monday through

Thursday mid-day. My employer paid my expenses while I traveled back and forth from the east coast.

When I first got to Houston I was trying to learn my way around the city after work and got a little lost. I remember going to a super market near the hotel I was staying. I exited the super market parking lot, turned on to the main road and came to a stop light where I was to turn right. While waiting for the light turn, I looked all around the area, and then I looked straight ahead. I saw the huge building and a big sign saying Riverview Church. I was in such shock and cars starting honking their horns at me to go through the light. I had to pull over and just stare at the building. Immediately my prayer from years before came to my remembrance. I had asked to be able to visit the church at least once and also to not pay to go visit. I had such a praise break and a laugh. For the next 2 ½ years I went to every Wednesday night service. That was the highlight of my week every week to attend the service. To this day I listen to Riverview Church services every week on line and now on satellite radio. I knew God heard my prayers but this was so amazing.

    When on my routine trip to Houston one week, right after I landed and while waiting at the baggage claim, I get a phone call from the lawyer's office in Grenada. By this time they are like family since I spoke to them so often. The clerk on the phone asked me if I saw my email. I said no, since my phone was off while I was in the air and I had just landed. I put in my blue tooth and I said hold on I will look now. I pulled up my email and my eyes started to tear up and I said to the person on the phone am I seeing correctly. A copy of the deed was sent to me and it was on my mother's birthday in 2013. October 21, 2013 I received the deed to the land. I told them I had to call them back. I got my luggage and I went straight to the bathroom in the airport. I went into a stall and I just cried and cried and had my thank you JESUS moment. I know I had church up in that bathroom stall and I know the people in the bathroom were wondering what was going on but I had to stop and give praise. I could not contain myself. That was such a wonderful moment. I could feel my Mom being a part of the cheering squad for me in heaven.

-Therefore we also, since we are surrounded by so great a cloud of witnesses, let us lay aside every weight, and the sin which so easily ensnares us, and let us run with endurance the race that is set before us, looking unto Jesus the author and finisher of our faith, who for the joy that was set before Him endured the cross, despising the shame, and has sat down at the right hand of the throne of God. Hebrews 12:1-2

Chapter 17

As I reflect back I tried to determine how I came up with the thought and or strategy to save my lunch money for obtaining my goal and pack my lunch over the years. This is with the understanding that God is a master strategist and everything I have is because of him.

I remember this story as if it were yesterday. When I was in 3rd grade the school I attended, like so many other schools at that time, sold plants and gifts for special occasions for the students to purchase. This particular time I'm mentioning was around Mother's day. All week I had been meaning to ask my parents for a few dollars to get a gift for my mother. Somehow it just kept slipping my mind and I would only remember after I got to school, ahhhh. Now it was the Friday before Mother's day and once again I forgot to ask for some money. During these days there was not an electronic way to receive money on my debit and or credit card, and there was definitely not a way to text. I did however have lunch money. I was starving that day and could not wait for lunch and as I walked to the cafeteria for lunch I passed the area where the Mother's Day items were being sold. It was either lunch or a gift for Mom. I had to make a decision. As hungry as I was that day, I just kept thinking about how much I wanted to give my Mom something that I saw for her at that school. I could just smell the golden brown french fries waiting for me to bite into them. I decided to buy the gift, I knew my Mom would love the gift just because I gave it to her. I knew she would love me even if I didn't get the gift for her from school and she would be happy if I made her something. I bought the gift and I was very happy with my decision. I knew my Mom would have something waiting for me after school to snack on before dinner. That's just how she was and I wanted to show my appreciation. I don't even know what happened the rest of the school day. I just put the gift up safely in my school bag and blanked out the rest of the school day. I was counting the time until the bell rang to end the school day and catch the school bus. When I got home I ate something……. I remember thinking that I was able to set a goal and achieve the goal by focusing and not being distracted by my current circumstance.

On mother's day I gave my Mom the gift I bought for her at school. I can still see her eyes light up and tear up. I loved seeing her happy. I loved being able to give her the gift. I remember my Mom asking me how did I buy the gift and I told her I used my lunch money. She then asked me how did I eat lunch and I told her I didn't. I told her I forgot to ask for a couple of extra dollars and I used what I had for lunch to get her the gift. The look on her face was something I will not forget as well, when Mom realized I chose not to eat lunch to be sure to get her a gift. It was worth being a little hungry to get my Mom something special.

Fast forward; when I first began to think about how to build the house in Belmont, I just had no idea of where to begin. I could not think about where the extra money would come from? Things were so tight at the time and I had no money to spare. How could I have this big dream to build this house, how would this goal be funded? I remember God bringing this 3rd grade story back to my remembrance. That concept was the basis of how I was able to start building. I bought groceries weekly, and I had to cook for myself and my daughters anyway, so I would pack leftovers or something from the house for my lunch every single day. I would write down the plan and modify it as needed. I found out the cost of the sand, stone, steel, concrete blocks and labor, and I saved towards each one of those items with my "lunch money". Essentially I was paying myself whatever I would have spent on lunch. I monitored everything I bought because I was on a mission. This strategy all came from the situation from wanting to buy my Mom a mother's day gift. This taught me and still teaches me to this day, that God uses all of your circumstances. Several scriptures come to mind:

1. I can do all things through Christ who strengthens me. Philippians 4:13

2. Trust in the lord with all thy heart, and lean not unto thine understanding. In all thy ways acknowledge him and he shall direct thy path. Proverbs 3:5-6

3. All things work together for good to them that love God and are called according to his purpose. Romans 8:28

This house is more than a house. This house is obedience to God and is to be used to help fund the growing of the Kingdom of God. Again, this is part of my purpose and to work towards being a philanthropist to make a positive meaningful difference in the Kingdom. Tears still come to my eyes every time I remember this part of the story, even now as I write this chapter, tears come to my eyes.

I still have the gift that I gave to my Mother that year. Every once in a while I take a look at it and remember her smile.

Chapter 18

Now that the land was free and clear, there was plenty of work that needed to be done to move forward with completing the house. Due to the house just sitting there for essentially 10 years, some materials needed to be replaced and a lot of new materials needed to be purchased. I received the estimate for building the roof of the house and it was both astonishing and staggering.

Once again I wrote down every detail of what needed to be done and the cost. I carried my book with me everywhere, writing any idea that came to my mind. The amount of money needed for the roof was so far out of reach I just pushed the dream to the back of my mind. I did not know how I could possibly come up with this money. Part of the dream is to not borrow for this dream house. This property was to be free and clear of any loans or liens. I tried borrowing from the bank and that was a disaster. I could not get a loan at all. No bank would allow me to borrow in the US for an investment in another country. The banks in Grenada wanted to get a charge over the entire free and clear land and required all sorts of crazy fees. I basically gave up trying to do it on my own.

A couple of years later I was watching a sermon on TV and a pastor spoke about starting a dream again and not giving up. He kept saying begin again, begin that dream again. It's not too late to begin again. I thought and felt him speaking directly to me. He said maybe you have a dream that God put in your heart. Stop making excuses he said. If God put it in your heart he will provide a way……Every promise and dream God put in your heart that you know you should be pursuing…you know you should begin again. I got chills. Begin again is all I heard over and over again. My husband Kevin said to me, this was just for you to hear.

    I thought to myself, could I really begin again, could I finish. What about the money for the roof. We now have kids in college and we ourselves were just finishing our Masters degrees another miracle at our age, but we did it. I prayed and said oh God I have no idea how to tackle this but I will begin and believe you will make a way. About 2 weeks later a good friend of mine that I have known for over 30 years called me and said, did you get a letter from Distinction Corporation about your pension? I said no. She said a few people who used to work for Faith Corporation, where we worked many years ago received letters from the new owners about getting a check. I said well that would be nice but neither one of us got a letter from them. A week after that call, sure enough both Kevin and myself received a letter from the new owner of the company we used to work for, writing about our pensions. The letter in summary said, as the new owner of the company they did not want to maintain the pensions for previous employees and we had 30 days to decide if we wanted the funds distributed to us directly or rolled over into another account not handled by them. Well my portion was more than enough to pay for the roof. It was not a large pension since I only worked there 11 years but it was more than enough for me to complete the next phase of the building project plus. Kev used his portion to purchase an investment property to gain another revenue stream and residual income for our household. He also used a portion of his funds to contribute towards additional materials and labor needed for the project.

From that time on, there has been nothing but favor after favor with the finishing of the house. The roof was completed and looks amazing. This came about after I handed over what needed to be done to God and stopped trying to do this roof on my own abilities. There are 15ft ceilings throughout the house. This was really astonishing to me. I believed all things were possible with Christ Jesus and I was able to witness miracles signs and wonders with this process. I made payments to the lumber company and the galvanize company. It was now time to take a break and just enjoy the moment.

Kevin and I flew down to see the roof on the house. I did not know how I was going to react when I saw it. Once we got off the plane the anxiety began to take hold.

This was not a bad anxiety this was excitement and humbleness and just being in awe to actually see with my own eyes the roof that was now finished. The roof that I had no idea how it could be possible to get done was completed. As we drove up the dirt road we could see the green roof glistening against the bright blue sky. I was a beautiful work of art that pictures could not do it justice. I was so thankful for this blessing and it was nothing but a gift from above. I knew I could do nothing without God and his hand was all in this gift.

After walking all around, with my notebook in hand, I always carried my notebook. Everything had to be documented, every idea, every drawing…it was all in the notebook. What would I do without my notebook? I always wrote down my dreams and my goals. Short term and long term goals. I would highly recommend writing down your goals. Let me back up, first think of your goals and then write them down. You have to be working towards something, otherwise what is your purpose. What are you working towards? What are you trying to achieve? Write the vision and make it plain – Habakkuk 2:2, this is biblical but it is also the basis of a business plan which leads towards achieving your goals. Every milestone should be and was celebrated as the house was built.

These were the major categories and each one posed their own set of challenges. The goal was to keep going and to be debt free. When the finances were not there then the work was stopped until we could save up all over again and again. Praise God for each step. This is the process I used to complete the house.

The next thing on the list was to get an estimate or two or three for the windows. When I received the estimate I was floored. I am not even sure how much I thought it should be but it ended up being a lot. My friend Amanda told me, girl look at that roof. She said if you were able to put the roof on, you will be able to get the windows purchased and installed. This is why we all need positive people in our lives that will encourage us along the way. Thank goodness for my wonderful husband who also encouraged me with this dream. We joined together as one, to focus on our desired goal of mentoring ministry. This dream would not be possible or it would be extremely difficult if your spouse is in disagreement with the dream, since large amounts of dollars are being directed outside of the home. Kevin and I are walking along this goal together, we work well together and we are friends that like one another. Yes we love each other and are married, but we also like each other and being around each other as friends.

When time came to purchase the tiles for the inside of the house, Kevin and I had a certain budget that we were working with for this purchase. We went to numerous stores on the island looking for the perfect tile with the perfect price. We said God you know our budget and we pray for favor. Our thought at the time was to purchase tile for most of the bedrooms, hallway, living room, dining room and kitchen. The tile we found that we loved, was on sale that week. We were not only able to tile the rooms we wanted but we were able to tile the entire house, plus we had left overs that were enough to tile the future downstairs apartment. This was a five loaves and two fish miracle. (Praise break). Mark 6:41

We were also able to purchase 7 security doors on sale. When we went to look for the spindles for the verandah, there happen to be a 50% off sale on the ones we wanted since there was a small defect with the mold that made the spindles. They were being discontinued. The spindles had a nick on the back where no one would be able to see except the builder, Kevin and I. This was favor over and over and I knew this was divine intervention.

Chapter 19

In September 2017 some of the most devastating hurricanes passed through the Caribbean. Hurricane Harvey, Irma and Maria were catastrophic storms. During these hurricanes I was up all night praying and crying and walking the floors. Hurricane Maria went through the Caribbean and left a lot of devastation in its path. What a scary scary situation. I listened to the local island radio stations for as long as they had power. Many prayers were going up that night. The island of Grenada was spared and it was evident it was spared by God. The islands to the North East of the island were hit very hard. At daylight after the storm, the damage to many of the Caribbean countries was monumental and visible.

People and nations from all over helped those that were impacted. Shortly after the hurricane I heard God clearly say to me to call my Uncle Cornelius in Saint Croix and check on him. At first I thought I must of heard wrong. I then heard it again without a doubt, and I thought you must be kidding oh God. Call my Uncle who tried his best to harm me and who has such hatred for me. I felt like a finger was on me saying call him. I mentioned this to my husband and my daughter Nina and both of them just looked at me. I said I can't shake this feeling. AHHHHHHHH I could not believe this mandate. I was not even sure if I still had his phone number. I had been in contact with so many family members during and after the storm to check on them. Everyone knew someone who had either been killed or experience massive losses on certain islands. I saw lots of videos of the devastation that were being passed around the Caribbean community. I sent a text message to a cousin of mine and asked him if he had our Uncle Cornelius's number. He was shocked that I asked for the number, but so was I actually. He gave me his house number and his cell number but so many people did not have electricity. There I was with these 2 numbers and I just starred at the numbers for a while.

I sat in my home office with my arms folded and just thinking to myself, I cannot believe I have to call my Uncle Cornelius. I looked up at the ceiling and I said okay God I'll do it. I felt like Joseph in the bible who had been betrayed but then took care of his family members who were so horrible to him. I dialed the number but I was really hoping he did not answer the phone. After the third ring, he answered the phone. The

TV in the family room went to mute. I knew Kevin and Nina muted the TV to listen since they could not believe what was happening. Keep in mind I had plans to never engage in any interaction with my maternal Uncles again. It took me about 10 or 11 years to completely forgive them and I thought okay I have forgiven them and life would just go on, but….

Forgiveness…

1. And be kind to one another, tenderhearted, forgiving one another, even as God in Christ forgave you. Ephesians 4:32
2. For if you forgive other people when they sin against you, your heavenly Father will also forgive you. But if you do not forgive others their sins, your Father will not forgive your sins.

Now I am in my home in my office and calling my Uncle Cornelius's number after the hurricane to check on him and he answered the phone. I said chupzzzz to myself. He said hello… I stuttered I said hello…. I did not know if I should call him Mr. Joseph or Uncle Cornelius, so I said hello this is Sandra, Eudalyn's daughter. I was calling to check on you to see if you were alright after the hurricane. He said Sandra, my niece Sandra. Oh Sandra thanks for calling, he then proceeded to tell me all of what has happened at his home and how they have no running water, that they are using buckets to get water out of the cistern and so on. I asked him if there was anything I could do to help him, but there was no way to ship or fly anything there. He told me he did not need anything at the moment. He thanked me for the call and said perhaps this is the door to us being able to communicate. He asked me for my cell number and asked me about the girls. I found the entire conversation unbelievable but I obeyed by calling. I told him I would call back in a few days to check on him and he said okay.

When I came out of the office Kev and Nina just looked at me and Kev asked me if I was okay. I said yes and went upstairs and just sat on the bed for about an hour. A couple days later I called my Uncle Cornelius back and he told me of all of the devastation on the island. There was no way for me to send anything but he was fine he said. We did not continue the communication afterwards.

Chapter 20

In April of 2018 Kevin and I went to Grenada and we were able to stay in our home for the very first time. There were a few things that needed to be adjusted but we were able to stay in the house. It was a true blessing. We had errands to run every day while we were there and as we were driving down the hill on this particular day, Kev said to me hold up hold up. I hit the brakes and asked what was wrong. He said there is a sign on the ground in the bush saying land for auction. I put the vehicle in park and pulled up the hand brake and we got out of the vehicle. Right in front of our property in the brush was the sign. I took a picture of the sign and we began to call the number on the sign. After about the 4th time calling someone answered the phone. I gave them my name and told them I was calling about the land up for auction in Belmont. The auctioneers name was Juan Lopez. Mr. Lopez asked me where I was located since he had several pieces of land up for auction in the Belmont area. I explained where we were located and he was then able to tell me about that particular piece. He said the auction was in two weeks and the starting bid was $101,000.00 CBD dollars, (Caribbean dollars). He explained that at the time of the auction the winning bidder had to pay 10% of the final bid immediately and then within 30 days pay the balance or forfeit the original 10% deposit. If the balance was not paid in 30 days from the winning bid then the land would go back up for auction and the original bidder would be obligated to pay for lawyer fees and the cost to re auction the property.

We just sat there in the vehicle for a few minutes trying to digest what we just heard. This was the land right in front of the property. In other words the land would be continuous. It was the same land that originally belonged to my Uncle Cornelius. He sold this particular piece of property after the court case was completed. He said in court that he was going to sell the rest of his property that surrounded the piece he initially gifted to my Mom to prevent me from ever having the ability to expand as my mother had asked years ago. All of this flashed in my mind. I said to Kevin, remember the person that bought this piece lived in Anguilla, the place where the hurricane hit. We then drove off to finish our errands.

Later that evening we discussed the land and we definitely could not come up with the money in two weeks, but we came up with a plan a, b, and c to see if we could get a loan. I think I was almost in a panic thinking that this is a possibility and it was going to not be attainable. Over the next week we tried to get a loan with a few banks on the island but the issue was we did not live there and we did not want to have the bank hold the current land and house we owned, as collateral. I'm sure the bank would be very happy to take a charge on that property and they were just a little too anxious to want to do that. There were so many phone calls to the banks and then a couple of appointments with a few banks and it all came to the same point that we needed to actually live on island etc. When we reached back to the States I tried to get a loan using one of the investment properties we had to no avail. After trying so hard to make this work, I just put my head down because I was all out of ideas and I prayed and ask God what should I do. I thought this was something for me but I could be wrong. I prayed and said I'm okay if this other piece is not for us oh God. We already had a lovely piece of land and the house was completed enough for us to be able to stay in it when we visit and or have short term rentals to tourist. Only the external fencing and some landscaping needed to be completed. I had made my peace but I just felt a tugging like I should not give up.

I hired a lawyer to represent me at the auction and I called the lawyer a couple of days before the auction and let her know I was officially withdrawing since I could not come up with the funds. The lawyer that was going to represent me at the auction was the same lawyer that handled my land case with my Uncle Cornelius. We both thought this would really be something if it had worked out. The day of the auction I remember praying and asking God if it possible and if it was his will that things would work out regarding the auction of the land. The auction was scheduled to begin at 1:00 pm on the land itself. I remembered that I kept looking at the time throughout the day. When 1:00 came I just tried to imagine what was happening. I called the lawyer at 1:45 and asked if she knew if the property was sold. She said I'll make a call and get back to you shortly. 15 minutes later the phone rang and I saw the lawyers name and number displayed on my phone. I answered the phone; hello I said. The lawyer said no one showed up for the auction. It was not sold. I could not believe it…it was not sold. I then called Kev and he said this is for you, you are being set up by God.

Over the next few days I made several phone calls trying to get an idea of when the land would possibly go back up for auction. I had to begin to plan how I would get this money whenever it was going to be back on the schedule. I read over and over Proverbs 3:5-6, Trust in the lord thy God with all thy heart and lean not onto your understanding. In all thy ways acknowledge him and he will direct your path. Every sermon I heard, every thought I had just kept saying trust me, trust me.

I spoke to this mountain and the word of God said if you have faith of a mustard seed… Mathew 17:20 And Jesus said to them, Because of your unbelief; for assuredly, I say to you if you have faith as a mustard seed, you will say to this mountain, Move from here to there. And it will move; and nothing will be impossible for you.

In June I went back to Grenada with two of our adult children. Our goal was to have a nice vacation and to see the girls at the orphanage and to get the technology associated with the house such as Wi-Fi and the smart TV's set up. While at the house we see the auctioneer drive up on the property in front of the house with another gentleman with him and put a new auction sign back up on the property. He did not look at us on the verandah at all, he just put the sign in the ground and walked around the land and got back in his vehicle. Tiffany went down to the land and looked at the sign. What we did not know at the time was another sign was put up on a light post on the main road. I made the phone call to the auctioneer to find out the date of the auction and I was told July 27th. I really believed this land was for me and was a gift from God. I prayed and said to

God, you are the master strategist, I need the strategy to obtain this land if this is for me. I cannot do this without you oh God. I pray this prayer in Jesus name.

When we returned to the States I applied for an equity loan with another investment property that we had. I thought everything was working out and all would be fine. I submitted all of the paper work that was requested and then I paid for the appraisal. I was upset the appraisal fee could not come out of the loan…moving on. Unfortunately the appraisal came in a little lower than I expected. Meanwhile the time is ticking. Every day is a day closer to the auction date. I found out a few people have inquired about the land. I thought this was a tactic by the bank who wanted to pressure me into purchasing the property based on the proximity of the house to the land being auctioned. My fear was that someone would buy it and block my view since the land was in front of me. Imagine this land was purchased by my Uncle Cornelius in 1960 and to this day he has never done anything with any of the acres that he has up on that hill. There is nothing but bush on the land and now he is more senior in age.

I was able to refinance an investment property at a lower interest rate and for less years, which was a huge plus but I was only able to walk out with the cash of $11,000.00 US which was $29,700.00 CBD. That left me short quite a bit and I would not be able to go to settlement until after the day of auction. I thought about my 403b but I already had one loan on that and based on that particular plan I was not able to take out more than one loan. I thought of paying off the loan since it was not an exceptional amount, and then re taking out a loan to make up the difference but based on the time frame I would need a few months and that was not going to work in this particular case. Keep in mind the funds from the 403b are mine, so any loan from the 403b is a loan from myself.

Prior to the auction I needed to make sure the lawyer had at least 10% of the asking price and maybe a little more in her account. I wired the 10% of the starting bid and sent a required explanation letter, to be presented to the bank stating the money was for the auction.

The day of the auction came and I called the lawyer in the morning to make sure everything was okay. The bidding was scheduled to start promptly at 1:00 pm. My lawyer arrived at 12:45 and she text me that there was another person there, an Italian woman. 15 minutes later she text me that another person had arrived for the bidding. There ended up being a total of 4 persons at the site to bid for the property. My lawyer text me to "CALL NOW". My heart started to beat so fast. I dialed the phone and paced. The auctioneer was reading the rules and then Italian lady started asking all kinds of questions. She wanted the land. The auctioneer said we are ready to begin. The bid started at $101,000 CBD. My lawyer said $101K and the Italian woman said $102K, We said $103K she said 104K I asked can we say $104,500. The answer was no, we can only bid in increments of 1000.00 I had given the lawyer a max of 108,000 CBD and thank goodness I was on the phone with the lawyer since we had to go over that amount. The other candidates had dropped out by then. We went back and forth and was extremely tense. The Italian lady said she had cash, she was asked to make a bid if she wanted to continue. She said $110,000 EC and I took a deep breath and told the lawyer to bid $111,000 CBD. Going once, going twice, SOLD. Yessssss praise God yessssss. I won the bid. Praise break……I called my husband and my dad and my friend Amanda. I was so excited. I had to immediately wire the balance for the deposit. Now the clock was ticking. I had 30 days to come up with the balance or I would lose the deposit, the land and have to incur additional fees. I tried so hard not to panic. I was working on the refinance of an investment property but I knew I it would not be enough. We could not sell property in time to meet the deadline either. I went into my prayer closet and started speaking the promises of God because I truly believed this was for me and as long as I lined up with God's will then it would work out, however I had to do my part.

While reviewing the paper work about the refinance for the investment property, I saw that I had to submit the terms of my 403b and submit the terms for withdrawing funds. I read the entire document and while reading I saw a clause that listed acceptable reasons for hardship withdrawals. One of the reasons was for the purchase of property. A light went off in my head, Bingo. I contacted the retirement plan company and asked what type of paper work would I need to submit for purchasing property and asked if the property could be outside of the United States. I then gathered the paperwork and sent it over. This allowed me to obtain the balance of the funds needed for the purchase of then land. There was not a loan, there was a withdrawal. This is how the land was purchased in full. Praise break. The land was paid in full.

While reading over the paper work from the lawyers and the bank that auctioned off the property I noticed the name of the previous owners of the land were on the document. The original owner was my Uncle Cornelius, who sold it to a lady on one of the neighboring islands. That particular island was heavily damaged during the last hurricane. The person who bought the land had defaulted on their payments and the bank repossessed the property. The land that my Uncle Cornelius purposely sold to prevent me from ever getting it ended up in my possession. That same week my Uncle Cornelius called me and I answered the phone and he said wanted to apologize to me. I said okay, I said apologize for what specifically and he then paused and then said for not calling you back last year after you called me about the hurricane.

Chapter 21

As we arrived with excitement for another trip to paradise, we anticipated seeing the house once again and preparing for our future guests by completing the finishing touches. We arrive, collect our bags and then pray as we go to face customs. This time we have composition books for the children at the church and some clothing items for the kids at the orphanage. With excitement we are cleared by customs to proceed. Ahhhh, back in Grenada… are my thoughts as we go into terminal. Kevin takes the 5 pieces of luggage and waits in the waiting area while I walk to the rental car section to pick up the reserved SUV. An SUV is definitely needed while we are on island since the road leading to our home has become worse by the day since we were last on island. We run our typical errands, going to the super market, picking up a meal or two and drinking water. As we pull up to the house with great excitement and calmness comes over me. The road is worse than I imagined and almost impassable. As we were driving up the hill I saw Greg the electrician working on the outside of the house. He was completing the installation of the new meter base. We greeted each other with a wave as we pulled into the garage. We immediately notice all of the excess tiles and building supplies in the upper left hand corner of the garage. Ahhhh I wanted this stuff removed and out of site since potential guest would not like to see these items. Kevin went into the house with the bags and I just looked at the edge of the driveway towards the sea. I then saw our neighbor up the hill, Boostie. Boostie, I said…..hey Sandra said Boostie as we walked towards each other.

We chatted for a few minutes and then I saw Derrick (the contractor) and a young lady walking up the hill. Hi Ms. Sandra! Hello how are you I responded. I was then immediately introduced to Tammy. I thought she was his family member and he said nooooo remember I talked to you about her as the person that does makeup. Our eyes met and I knew and he knew I was not told of this lady being his girlfriend. At the time, I thought she was there to visit with him at the apartment in which he occupies. Kev and I just kind of "lime" for some time and then started to unpack. We were a bit tired and then decided to pull out the TV's prior to going to bed. When we went into the closet to get out the TV's, they were not there. I thought hmmm did I put it somewhere else, or did Derrick move them for some reason. We quickly realized they were not in the house. I sent Derrick a text message asking him if he knew where the TV's were. Since I did not receive a response I walked down to the apartment and knocked on the door. When the door opened I asked about the TV's. I was asked what do you mean….. I said the TV's are not there as well as a 40 piece tool set that was in the closet. Derrick then came out of the apartment and walked very fast in front of me up to the main house. He looked around and stated he saw them the night before when he was putting up the TV mount. Derrick said the police need to be called. What is crazy is the TV's were wrapped in a moving blanket and in the walk in closet behind a few boxes. This was taken by somebody that was familiar with the house or had been to the house before. I called information to get the number for the local police station and then contacted the police. I gave the directions to the home….. It's a yellow concrete house with a green roof across from the old kitchen cabinet maker place. From a distance we saw the police coming towards the house within 5 minutes or so. However we saw them turn back around before turning up the hill. Ahhhh I called back the police and explained I saw them and tried to wave them up the hill. I told them to come up the hill, and I turned on all the outside lights. I saw the vehicle come back towards the house moments after I called. The officers parked in the driveway and approached the house looking at all of us so very carefully. I explained where the TV's were and when Kevin and I realized they were missing. Derrick walked with us along with the officers. The problem about the TV's missing is, nothing was broken into at the house. No broken windows or doors. The 6 entry doors were in tack. They all have a 3 tier dead bolt lock system. 3 locks in the side wall, 3 in the top of the wall and 3 into floor. This clearly meant it was an inside job. The police questioned Derrick asking who had a key or was given a key and so on. We were asked to come to the local station on Thursday, which was in two days. We were told the police will be investigating the electrician, house keeper and any worker that had been working on the home recently. The next morning we went down town to try and submit Kevin's citizenship papers which was one of our main reason for coming to the island on this particular trip. I wanted to add him to the deed of the land we just purchased via the successful auction bid. The fact that we were given the opportunity to purchase the land in front of our property was a pure blessing from God.

Before we left the states I copied all of the original documents as stated in the instructions or so I thought. We had to go to a lawyer, Judge or Magistrate to have the application notarized and on that island were we able to complete this task. I could not believe the fee was $100.00. I said I would never complain again about the $5.00 - $7.00 fee in the States. We then take the paper work to the passport office. When we walked in we were the only ones, excellent. We had to still sit and wait for our number to be called. When our number was called I gladly produced the documents as the representative called. The copy of my birth certificate was not accepted, since the signature at the bottom of the page was slightly cut off. The copy of my Mom's birth and death certificate was not accepted since her name was spelled differently on three of my documents. It was hilarious but this is what it was. We had to go to the high court to apply for a new death certificate, and we had to go to Inland Revenue to pay the fee of the citizenship application. Two different parts of town and then we had to be back at the passport office by noon to submit all of the requested documents or return the next day. Inland Revenue did not take too long to pay the fee, however the drive to Inland Revenue could be compared to an obstacle course with the roads being worked on and the giant holes to avoid. We then hustled over to the high court where we had to go to the window to request the death certificate in the spelling of the name that I have always known. I'm not even sure how my Mother had so many spellings of her name out there….. I completed the form and then submitted it and was told to wait in the reception area to be called. The time was just passing and passing. We still had to go and get the new photo copies of the papers that were not accepted by the passport office. I was getting more and more irritated by each passing minute.

We arrived around 10:00 am and not it was 11:00. I went up to the window to ask for a status and I could see my paper on the desk. I was told to wait a few more minutes. At 11:20 I asked where I could get photo copies made as requested by the passport office. I couldn't just sit there, I'm sure I was driving Kev crazy but I just needed to keep busy. I knew we had to go to the police station the next day and I didn't have time to sit in the passport office on Thursday to submit these papers. I was instructed to go down a long hallway and then to the number 3 window on the left. I asked the lady at the window if I could get copies made and she seemed as if I were bothering her. The lady at the window handed my paper to another lady to make copies who then slowly took out the stapes and then walked each paper over one by one to the copier machine. The 2nd and 3rd copy, she had to destroy by shredding on the other side of the room, and then return to try and copy again. Just before the last paper to be copied a co-worker of the representative asked if she could get some things copied right away and then my papers were put down and the ladies copies made.

I was infuriated but what could I do at this point. Finally the copies were made and I paid my money. At 11:45 almost 20 people were called up to the window to receive their documents. I could not believe they were all held in a pile and all called at once to be handed out. I thought, we might be able to make it. I got the paper and then Kevin said he had to go to the bathroom. I thought it may still be possible. I went to the window to get a copy of the revised document while he was in the rest room. It's now 11:55 and reality has hit me that we will not be making it to the passport office by noon. Even though it was 3 to 4 minutes away by car, we still had to walk over to the vehicle and then get out of our tight parking space, and then drive. It was not going to happen. Soon after we got home the police came up the hill to the house again for the 4th time. No complaints on our end since at home in the city we may not have even received an initial visit as yet. Greg the electrician was also waiting for us at the house and the police said they wanted to speak to Kevin and I in the house as they spoke with Greg in the garage. We were then told they were taking Greg the electrician to another village station since Derrick was at the local village station. The police wanted us to come and give a statement. Now keep in mind we did not know any of this would occur while planning this trip. Therefore I had faux locks in my hair and had scheduled an appointment to have my hair braided while in Grenada the next day. Since I had an appointment, I had started taking out my locks in preparation for washing my natural hair. Picture this; I am strategically taking out my hair so I can half way camouflage the craziness that is going on with my hair. I had to reschedule my hair appointment 3 times in total during this situation. I had the front right side on my hair in faux locks and the other sections natural. I was mortified that the police insisted we come down to the station while I'm looking real crazy. We ended up being at the station for over three hours. What a day. We were told Derrick was being held in the station as a prime suspect. He was being held since he was responsible for overseeing the home and nothing was broken into. We didn't' think Derrick would have stolen the items. I think he was set up by a worker or one of his girlfriends. He was definitely involved with more than one woman and it is dangerous to tamper with someone's heart strings. When we arrived the same girl Tammy was at the police station asking if we knew what was going on. The police told us she said she lives at my home with Derrick. I was shocked. We never knew this little fact. I took a deep breath and a sigh and wanted to know what was going on here.

We were then permitted to go home and I still just did not know what to think. As I walked through the house, looking at everything in detail, I realized the well pump and the hot water heater were missing as well. I was just so disgusted. Kevin and I work so hard to make this dream come true and somebody just literally walks in and walks out of the front door with our things thinking things somehow just fall out of the sky into this home. Not only do the items need to be re-purchased, they most likely will need to be driven from Connecticut to New York and then shipped internationally from New York. The items will need to be cleared through customs and then transported to the home. So much goes into this process. I am tired and about to go to bed when I get about three phone calls from Sean, the electrician who is working on the downstairs apartment electrical issues. I just cannot imagine why he is calling, calling, calling so much, so I finally answered the phone. He said he received a call from the prison that Derrick was asking for food. Apparently the jail at that location does not provide meals for prisoners. Sean said he did not have transportation and Derrick had not eaten all day. My first thought was what happened to the girlfriend that was there earlier. Kev and I just looked at each other and just could not believe this situation. I told Sean we would go and pick up something for him. I looked at the time and just put my head in my hands. The last place to get something to eat in the area was going to close in about 15 minutes. I gave Lolly's restaurant a call and asked if I could still place an order. We hurried in the car to drive down the hill and to pick up the order. We made it just in time. Now it was time to go to the local police station. I guess this will look real crazy that we are taking food for the person that is accused of stealing our things. At this point I did not what to think, I was exhausted. We pulled up to the police station and I waited in the vehicle as Kev went into the station to take the food and large bottle of water. The officer made Kev eat some of the food to make sure we did not try to poison Derrick. I had no more words… I just wanted to go home and try and get my mind together as to what is occurring and why. Why is this happening? This was to be such a great moment with purchasing the new piece of land and applying for citizenship. The next morning we got dressed early and picked up some breakfast for Derrick. We take the breakfast to the station and are told that he was moved to the prison in town but not the main one as yet. I thought really, was there evidence? None at all, just circumstantial since he was the caretaker. I believe he trusted someone and they betrayed him, which ultimately hurt Kevin and me. We drove down to the passport office to submit the papers. As we are driving, I realized I forgot to bring my change of shoes since I was wearing flip-flops. Flip flops were not permitted in the high court and I thought there may be an issue at the passport office. We decided to continue along the way since we were almost there. We get to the building and the only restriction for that location was no shorts and no sleeveless shirts. We were given our number and then finally up to the window. The papers were accepted. Yesssss At this point we are on the island day three and no beach as yet. We then go to Wavejet to clear the two boxed mattresses we shipped before we left. A few days before we arrived on island, I asked a broker, who I have known for almost 10 years, to get someone to clear the items from customs. The day we arrived, he said his contact told him it would be 1000.00 EC to clear the items. That did not sit well with me and I refused and said we would clear them ourselves. We were very familiar with the process and sometimes when people see things are coming from America they feel as though people in America as my dad would say; walk out each morning and pick money off of the trees. Chupzzzz. So here we are at the port which is located at the back of the airport. This is where cargo items can be flown into the island. We had the two mattresses flown in so we could have everything set up while we were actually on island. It's a timing thing as to which way to go with the shipping, cargo plane or cargo ship. The process is much to be desired.

First, we had to go to the Wavejet office and pay for the shipment since it was sent freight collect. Then we had to go to the customs office and show them paperwork from Wavejet. We then go to another customs area for them to pull the items from the warehouse and place a value. You then have to go back to the first customs area and provide the paper work of the established value and a percentage placed into the computer of what you are to pay. That paper work then goes to the customs cashier office to pay the fee. Now back to the first customs office where you are to show it has been paid. A signed paper is then given to you to take to the warehouse area. Once you return to the warehouse area and show all of that paperwork, you are free to take your items. Yes, it is a process and somehow I do not mind it and I find it fascinating. I think I could gladly do this as a job. I would be a broker and clear items for people. It's lucrative since most people cannot be bothered with this process. By us clearing the items ourselves, the cost was 400.00 CBD. I called Lionel, the gentleman that has handled the transportation of our building supplies for the past 10 years, to pick up the cargo. He said he was sending his son with his truck to collect and deliver the items up to the house for us. Thanks Lionel!!

As we were driving back home, the fingerprint department called to meet us at the house to take pictures of the scene and try and search for finger prints. We finally get home and let the officer in the house to process what they needed to process. About 20 minutes after the police leave, there is a knock on the door and it is Derrick's brother and girlfriend wanting to talk about the situation. I thought this is a long day that just never ends. I was seriously trying to figure out what in the world was going on in the spiritual world. What was the battle about? Was it the land that was just purchased and its potential to fund the philanthropic work that we planned?

Alfred, Derrick's brother asked if we could work out some sort of restitution regarding Derrick and his ability to get out of the jail. Kevin explained to Alfred that we did not place charges on Derrick and that we did not believe he was directly responsible; however, he had to be indirectly responsible since he was put in charge of overseeing the property and that somebody used a key to walk in a take out the items. I explained that there were two other items missing, the hot water heater and the well pump. I said if we mention that to the police it will add to his charges and be a bigger issue. Alfred asked for us to go to the jail down town and speak with the lawyer about making restitution. He said Derrick is not going to make it in the prison system. We agreed to go down town, of course they both wanted to ride down town with us to the prison. We stated we would be going down town but had things to do and they would need to find a way back into the countryside. I just needed a moment to get myself together…about 20 minutes later we were ready to get on the road.

By this time I was able to get my hair braided at some crazy hour the night before and tipped my hair braider very well for accommodating me. We were able to get a parking spot not too far from the entrance of the jail at the main police headquarters. Once we entered the building, Alfred spoke to an officer to grant us permission into the police prison area and speak to the court appointed lawyer. As we enter into the first gate, we see Derrick on the side office, being finger printed and he catches a glimpse of us passing the room. We enter into an inner courtyard where you are able to see various sections "cages" as they are called. There are cages that line the inner court and then an outer cage where a prisoner can come out from the main group in that respective area to speak with visitors, lawyers and or the police. We walk pass this cage area and go upstairs to what appears to be a dilapidated area where court appointed lawyers have their offices or meetings areas. We wait there for at least 40 minutes. There is a balcony that we can go out and overlook the inner court. Kevin and I go outside and at that time I realize the balcony that we are standing on, is made of wood strips and you can see the prisoners that are in the outer cage below us.

We finally meet with the lawyer and it comes down to us writing out a scope of work that will document the restitution that can be agreed upon for the items stolen. Upon this agreement, all of us, the lawyer, Derrick's brother, his girlfriend, Kevin and I, go downstairs to the cage area. The cage looked like a cage. The smell from the cage is shocking. The conditions are not as atrocious as the main prison, but it's not too far from it as well. To give you a better picture of the prison; there is not a septic infrastructure in the prison. They use the pail system. The questions are; does everyone get their own pail or do you have to share a pail, when is the pail emptied, and where is the pail emptied. That is the basic description and that should give you a good idea of the conditions. Family members and friends bring food to prisoners daily to eat. I'm not sure what happens to people who do not have someone to bring food to them to eat daily.

The lawyer went down to the cage to speak with Derrick about the plan. A court date was set for Monday. Monday on my birthday, what a thing. We were then able to speak to Derrick and we gave him some food that we bought. He looked real paranoid; it seemed as if he was trying to figure out how things got this far out of control and who is responsible for setting him up. My thoughts as well as Kev's is he, Derrick, does not want to mess up this gig he has with us. It works at this time but is not a permanent situation. He went back into the inner cage and we left the police station. Alfred and Tammy went their own separate ways.

We decided to do a little shopping while in town and then go and get some ice cream. We just needed to not focus on this theft situation for a few moments. We finally reached back home and planned to go to the beach for the afternoon. We really needed some us time, and time to decompress. Early Saturday morning Boostie knocks on the door to find out what is going on. She said she is willing to bail out Derrick and or go to court on Monday to testify for him. Derrick has done a lot of construction work for Boostie and always had the opportunity to pilferage through her things but did not. She had also recommended him to many of her friends. He was not a thief, he was however a womanizer.

Chapter 22

Sunday morning I went to the church my Mom used to pastor to take composition books, pencils and pens to the school age children. This was one the many philanthropic endeavors Mom and I and now Kev and I have planned. The goal is to help others in need, for others to know God can and will make a way. Kev and I were willing to be vessels to happily help others. I was so excited to give the items to the children. It brought such a happiness to me to do this. I wish I could do more, and Kev and I have plans to do so much more next year and in the future. The children were so happy to get the items. I loved seeing the look on their faces that someone thought of them. There were 26 students at the church. Next year we plan on giving each school-aged child a school bag, five composition books, pens, pencils and erasers. I'm excited about the plan and the kids have no idea. We will give the items much earlier in the summer so the parents will know how to budget themselves and not worry about those items. That evening my friend Sheria came by to visit me, but since the road was so bad, she parked at the bottom of the hill and I drove down to pick her up. We chatted about old times and I showed her around the house. We went down memory lane about when the house was started and my tenacity. We talked about her writing a book and I became so excited since I was in the process of writing one as well. We were going to keep each other accountable on writing. After her visit, I drove her back down the hill and there was a white car parked in the corner at the bottom of the hill. I initially ignored the car since these days some vehicles just cannot make it up the hill.

As Sheria and I sat in the vehicle at the bottom of the hill talking, someone got out of the white car and started walking towards my vehicle. At first I did not even realize someone was in the white vehicle, and the person came to the window of the drivers' side. They proceeded to show me their police officer badge stating there were investigating the missing TV's and monitoring the area. I thought that was so strange and just looked at the gentleman and said okay. Two minutes later Derrick's girlfriend gets out of the vehicle and says Ms. Sandra I'm sorry, this is my friend and they just gave me a ride home and I didn't want you to think something strange was happening in light of the situation. I just looked at them since all I was doing was talking to my friend. This is something you just cannot make up. I guess they thought we just sat there wondering who was in the vehicle and we had no idea they were even in the vehicle. I had to drive Sheria down the hill since her car could not make it up the hill, that's all. This whole situation was just so strange and real crazy in my opinion. It was one of those moments when you should simply shake your head and move on with your thoughts since there is nothing you can do about the situation at all.

Chapter 23

Monday morning and happy birthday to me. I received a call from the police reminding me that we had to go to court at 10:00 am and to dress properly. Well we brought vacation clothes so we had to do a little repeating to ensure we were dressed properly for court. We got up early that morning and drove into town to handle some business and then rushed back to St George to get to court. We parked in the "lot", a grass field, and then we walked over to the building. This is something that I have never experienced on the island. We see the investigating officer and ask if we are to wait outside at this location under the tree. He said yes until the door is opened and they call the case we wait on the benches outside or in the area where you can hear your name. Well it felt like 100 degrees outside…well well. Thank goodness the door was opened and they let a few people in and we made sure we were able to get in and sit down on one of the benches inside the courtroom. There were three rows of benches on both sides of the courtroom, each set was behind the prosecutor and the defending lawyer. There were also two wooden stands on either side, one for the plaintiff and one for the defendant. There is a clerk in the middle of the witness and defendant stands and then the Judge's bench up on a platform

The police officers were lined up against the wall of courtroom and in the middle of the aisle. There were so many people outside on the benches under the tree as well as all around the parking area. We could see them from the window inside the courtroom. We had no idea which case would be called, nor in what order, and I had a meeting with my lawyer to sign the final papers of the land at 12:30 pm. Kev would not be able to have his name on the papers until he obtained citizenship through our marriage. I was born in the Caribbean, however I have citizenship in Grenada as a descendant of my mother. We sat on the bench and to my right were three ladies and Kev sat on the end of the bench on my left. I think he is just trying to understand and adapt to the Caribbean culture. He's okay when people speak slowly but when the dialect takes on full action he is just out and cannot figure out what is being said. He will get there. One of the ladies sitting to my right said are you Ms. Sandra? Now my immediate question to myself is how does this lady know me? She said I recognize Mr. Kevin by his hair from your Messaging App picture. Chupzzzz and triple chupzzzz. This young lady then tells me her name and said she used to visit the apartment at my house with Derrick. Imagine that. She said they are no longer together but he called her and asked for her to come to the court today. Now this guy has two women at the courthouse, his ex and his current. The question is why am I finding out that she visited the apartment in the courtroom. I turned my head and whispered to Kevin what had just happened and we both looked at each other in amazement. She then says to me Derrick always talks about you and I hate to believe he would have done something like this after you have been so good to him. I'm sure he didn't do it. Now what are the chances of us sitting on the same bench as the lady and she recognizing us to speak to us? Life is really something. I kept looking at the time on Kev's watch since our phone had to remain off or at least on silent while in the courtroom.

There was a large monetary charge for anyone's phone going off while court was in session and instead of taking a chance of it being on silent and vibrating, I just turned it off. I had to watch the time since I had an appointment with my lawyer to sign the final land papers of the land that we just purchased a week prior to arriving on the island. At this point, I knew I would not make the scheduled time with my lawyer, so I stepped out of the courtroom to make a call outside in the hot hot sun. As I started to dial the number Derrick's current girlfriend walks up to me and asks, how is everything going inside and what is happening. I told her nothing has happened with him as yet, his name has not been called. Then the old girlfriend who was sitting next to me in the courtroom, comes up to me and I guess tries to have some sort of conversation with me but by now I have reached my lawyers' office on the phone and I am not able to have an outside conversation. I pause as the two ladies begin to fuss at each other, "don't speak to me one says to the other, me an you nah friend. I look at them both and say this has nothing to do with me, excuse me and I step away to begin my conversation with the law clerk. I tell the law clerk that I am not able to make the meeting at 12:30 pm and ask if it is possible to meet later today. They said they will check and call me back. I explain that I am in court and that I cannot keep my phone on. (I'll have to explain that later when I meet the lawyer). We agree to meet for 2:00 the same day since Kevin and I are scheduled to leave the island the next day. I then hang up the call, turn off my phone and go back into the courtroom.

As the cases are called, an officer goes to the door that leads to the outside field and calls out the defendant's name. Anybody that is there on their behalf as a witness or in any manner may now enter into the courtroom. As the inmates' cases are presented, they are brought into the courtroom and only at that time. One police officer stands to the left side of the Judge and another police office stands in front and slightly to the right side of the Judge. As each case is finished, the Judge says stand down to the defendant. A particular case that was heard before the one I was there for was about four young ladies who jumped one young lady. The young lady that was jumped had lots and lots of bandages all over her body. Three on her head, many on her arms, torso and so on.

The four defendants stood before the Judge. The girls had truly damaged the young lady and were all placed in prison for a week. They were all released on bail the Friday before court. The Judge asked a few questions and then proceeded to look at her cell phone. She pulled up a social media app, where she read out loud a post that one of the ladies posted right after they were bailed out of prison on Friday.

Now when the ladies received bail they were told to not contact the girl they jumped, neither directly or indirectly. One of the girls bullied the victim through social media and therefore the Judge told her she revoked her bail. The other three young ladies were told to stand down and they did as they walked out of the court room free, with fear in their eyes. The lady whose bail was revoked fell out on the floor begging the Judge for mercy. The police pleaded with her to get up. Get up they said get up. The girl said your honor I have a son please your honor I did not post that statement. Now clearly she did. She was removed from the courtroom. She was later brought back into the courtroom now and she was very humble. The Judge ordered the young lady to the stand and spoke harshly to her. The Honorable Judge stated, after watching the behavior you demonstrated in this courtroom today, I am sure I made the right decision and I am also holding you in contempt of court. She was remanded until mid- January. Derrick Blair's name was then called. My name was called as well. I was asked to step outside for a few minutes by the prosecutor. I was asked if I was dropping the charges, and I answered yes. I'm not sure why Kevin's name was not called. I then was told to go to the witness stand. It's literally a stand in a white painted box… I heard, do you promise to tell the truth and the whole truth so help you God as the Bible was held. I said I do. This country believes in God by the way. The Judge asked me is it Ms. Williams or Mrs. Williams, I said Mrs. I have no idea if that even mattered but I was not about to ask. I was asked what was my stance. I had already written the letter and sent it to the lawyer. I said we have agreed to Derrick providing restitution. I was then asked if I was threatened and coerced and I answered no. Derrick was told he was free and to stand down. Next case… we left the courtroom quickly. Outside of the courtroom Kevin, Derrick, Derrick's brother, his current girlfriend and myself all stood in a circle and talked. Derrick's ex was summoning him, he turned and said one moment. I said Derrick I do not know if you believe in God but I said a prayer for you. I wanted to plant the seed in him that God is real and in everything. The Holy Spirit can do the rest with the situation. I was not sure how all of them were getting back down the road but we had things to do. Kevin wanted to go home, so I dropped him off, chilled for a moment and then drove into town to meet the lawyer. Only I could sign the papers at this time since Kevin's citizenship is not final as yet. We are hoping to have his citizenship approved soon in order for his name can go on the land as a co-owner. I think this would give him a sense of being more a part of the land in Grenada. His name will be on the document and as my husband who also contribute to this journey I believe his name should be on the land and I look forward to that day.

Chapter 24

If things aren't tough enough Kevin and I had a huge problem with some tenants in the US that have not paid their rent in months, are challenging to say the lease in their personality and behavior and refuse to leave our property. I'll call the tenants Rashad and Shantee, the Irvin Street tenants. This particular relationship started out well, and slowly went very much down-hill to non-existent. They were always late and partially paid many times to the point it was hard to keep track. This would be a lesson learned. Business and niceness does not always mix well. The first time we tried to evict these tenants was when the lateness and or non-payment of the rent got out of control. A month or so before we filled the eviction court papers, since the eviction letter asking them to leave did not work, there was a flood in the basement. Ahhhh can you believe this. They had clothes everywhere and I mean everywhere. You could not walk in that basement without walking over some article of clothing and you definitely could not see the basement floor. I was trying to figure out if it was old clothing or winter clothing or if they didn't believe in washing clothes and just kept buying new clothes. The flooding stemmed from the tenants flushing non-biodegradable wipes down the toilette. Shortly after the flooding of the basement of this property we began our formal eviction attempt for these tenants. We sent a letter to the tenants asking them to vacate the premises due to non - payment of rent. On the day of court both tenants showed up and told the Judge we did not initially have a renter's license and therefore they were not obligated to pay rent during that time period where the license lapsed nor were they obligated to pay the outstanding 1000.00 water bill. They did have to pay the rent from the day we filed with the court since our renters license was renewed when we filed the court papers. The tenants paid the rent shortly before the Sherriff was scheduled and we were obligated to allow them to stay in the property until their lease ended. Fast forward, the same tenants are still in the house and we were notified of a leak in the roof. We hired a roofer to patch the roof and a couple of months later we get another call that the roof is still leaking and the kitchen roof has caved in, onto the kitchen floor. The odd thing is when you look at the damage you cannot see up to the sky. There was a leak by the window and the water damaged the ceiling tile. The front enclosed porch leaked as well. This place and tenants were just too much of a hassle. We went back and forth about when a good time would be for us to come into the property (our naivety at the time to even ask). Weeks later Rashad notified us he paid for a mold test and was waiting for the results. He said he refused to pay rent for a mold infested property. I just could not imagine that the property had been mold infested. What in the world had happened in that house? When we got the report from the lab, I suppose Rashad and Shantee were hoping it had been worse than it was. The report stated the basement had mold. The tenants never cleaned up the wet clothes after the flood. How could they have left all of those wet clothes in the basement?

Somehow they had it in their messed up heads that we were to clean up their clothes from the basement. We should have inspected the house on a regular basis. This is another lesson learned. Fast forward again, we went to court once again to evict these tenants. We eventually got the writ of possession which is the approval to evict the tenants and take back ownership of the property. When we were able to enter the property after the Sherriff secured the house, the tenants left everything in the house and pooped in the bath tub. The way I viewed this situation was, it is a preparation for our future goal of owning an apartment building. We will make sure we have a detailed business plan for that project and business. We will run a tighter ship so to speak. This was a distraction that we refused to distract us from accomplishing our overall goals. All of these things were taking place at the same time. It felt like we were popcorn in a popcorn popper. Things were popping off all over the place.

Chapter 25

My life was going in so many directions simultaneously. I felt as if I were being challenged in every area of my life, every area.

While the house in Grenada is going on, issues at our church were occurring and what was to be my safe place, my holy place of public worship, had been infiltrated by unhappiness and cliques and major church hurt. For a little background of myself. I am preacher's kid. Many of us have had church hurt and I am no stranger to this since I am a preacher's kid twice over. Both of my parents were pastors. My father is a retired minister. Two Uncles on my mother's side are pastors and my mother's father was a part time pastor and a "medicine man". On my father's side I have another Uncle that is a pastor and my paternal Grandfather was a part time pastor as well as painter. With this type of background I have been privy to the reality of people and the behind the scenes of church and it is not always pretty. As a preacher's kid you are held to a high standard. At some point you realize that many people in the church and the world, who put on the face of perfection, are far from perfect behind closed doors. The possession of this knowledge can be horrific. This has made it very difficult for me to have many friends. My circle of good friends is very small. It is difficult for me to trust people, and right, wrong or indifferent, I keep most people at an arm's length. I'm sure I've witnessed hundreds of weddings and funerals and let's says reality awakenings of parishioners.

During the past few years I was honored with the opportunity of an adjunct professor position at the same University I received both of my Master of Science degrees. My husband and I both graduated with our first Master's degree together. That was an exciting day and a day neither one of us thought would of happened. Our parents and children were able to see us graduate and I only wish my Mom would have been there to see me walk across the stage. I think she would be shocked but extremely proud. She always wanted me to finish school and I promised her I would go back one day and finish, and I kept my promise.

One day while at my day job, on what appeared to be a normal day, an unusual meeting was placed on my calendar. At this point in time, I loved my job and I constantly looked for ways to improve processes and functionality within the various applications my team and I implemented, upgraded and maintained.

I went into the office for this unknown meeting. When I reached the meeting room, my immediate boss was also in the office. I was a bit alarmed and quickly tried to assess the situation. I just took a deep breath and listened. My boss, Jill, had just submitted her resignation. I was in complete shock, and she was a great boss that taught me many things. I felt as if I were being groomed for her position all along. Whenever she was out of the office or even sometimes while she was in the office, I could easily fill in for her at meetings. I had fully immersed myself into the organization to learn as much as possible about the inner workings.

On the flip side her position was now available and I was looking forward to applying for her position. My counter-part, Tom, was also interested in her position and indicated he would apply as well. Tom and I spoke and it was known between us that we would both be seeking the position. I thought this would be a great opportunity for me to become a Director of the department. I had poured so much into the job and I believed I met most of the qualifications. One of the pre-requisites for applying for the position was the candidate must have a Bachelor's degree and a Master's degree was preferred. I thought at a minimum Tom would not be a qualified contender since he did not have a Bachelor's degree. We both went through the interview process and potential candidates outside of the organization were interviewed as well.

Finally, I was called into the office by leadership for a meeting. I said this is my day, Kev and I were excited about this new endeavor, I thought this would help us with our dreams and goals to move forward quicker, look at how God was opening this door I said and I was elated. I had all kinds of plans for the department to continue to make us successful within the organization. I got all dressed up professionally of course, and I walked into the secretary's office who greeted me kindly as usual. I was then escorted into the main office and I did my best to calm my nerves. I was thanked for coming in and then I was told I am sorry but we have selected another candidate. Tom is the new Director of the department. I thought I was hearing things. In my head I said are you kidding me. I was told that although I had the educational qualifications, they thought that my standards were too high and that no one would be able to keep up with me and that I was too rigid for the staff.

They said I scored well on the interview and Tom scored a **.5** higher than me. I squirmed in my chair from side to side. I thanked him for allowing me the opportunity to even interview for the position and then it was over. I opened the door and I left and went immediately to my car. I held in my tears for as long as I could, since I have a rule to never cry in front of the people at work. I will never let them see when they can push my buttons.

As soon as I got in the car, I calmly drove out of the parking lot and called my husband. He answered the phone and said congratulations Ms. Director. My heart sunk and I just broke out in tears at that point. I said no babe, they told me I was not selected. He said I am so sorry babe. I was distraught. I could not believe that Tom was selected. No degree and a Caucasian male. I actually overheard Tom at a later date laughing that he could not believe he got the position and that he did not even have to get a degree to get it. The field I work in is a male dominated field, however women and making huge strides.

Now I'm not saying you need a degree to do all jobs, I am saying that if it is a requirement then it should be a requirement.

My thoughts are I did not blend into the current landscape to move up any further, and for whatever reason I thought those details would not matter. I just did not get it, since at one of my previous jobs I was told I needed a Bachelor's degree to move up the ladder. When I received my Bachelor's degree my manager and director at that time did not acknowledge that degree. I was told by my Manager to remove my comments in my annual evaluation regarding the completion of my degree. Once he said that I spoke to Human Resources and they stated it was a major deal and should be mentioned in my evaluation. My bosses then told me they did not realize I graduated with my Bachelor's degree. Keep in mind the company paid for the degree but my bosses at that time stated they did not know.

I moved to another company shortly after that, which I loved and it permitted me to fully utilize my talents. Unfortunately after almost three years, the traveling became too much for both my family and myself and it was best to move on to another chapter. I then moved to another job where I obtained both of my Master degrees and again my degrees do not matter, nor are they acknowledged. In fact I was specifically told at this job, that degrees do not matter unless you are a clinician. I actually had staff that have degrees and the organization does not even acknowledge their degrees as an asset as well. The Human Resources department at this job does not recognize all degrees in their records. This still bothers me to this day. This is the reality, you cannot force people to accept you and or your credentials. Sometimes it's just a personality situation and has nothing to do with credentials. Sometimes you are not the right candidate. I tell my adult children to use me as an example and do not allow anyone to minimize them or their degrees. My husband Kevin always told me, "your job does not validate you". He would constantly speak that into my life and it encouraged me immensely.

Psalm 75: 6-7 "For exaltation comes neither from the east nor from the west nor from the south. But God is the Judge: He puts down one, and exalts another." This position was not for me and God did not open this door for a reason. This is something I must accept and move on from. What God has for me it is for me and this new role I was trying to obtain was not part of God's plan for me.

I did not have the pressure that I saw Tom faced day after day. I made sure I started work on time, took lunch breaks and ended the day on time as well. I also did not stay up at night worrying about issues at work. Thankfully, my department leadership management team as a whole worked very well together.

After Tom took the position, I applied for numerous jobs that entire calendar year and Unfortunately/fortunately I could not land any one of those jobs. I was asking God why and what is going on here, and I was confused, since I thought I was doing my part. This was a humbling experience. In the meantime I was thankful for the job. I worked with a great staff and intended to continue to do my best at the job for as long as I was there.

I threw myself into strategizing how to finish the house in Grenada and get things moving forward. I flew down to Grenada over and over to organize everything. I was on the island almost every other month making "moves" so to speak. I learned to not only thank God for the doors that he opens but also the doors that he has closes. God is able to see the entire picture of your life. Because this door closed I had less stress at work and was easily able to focus on my project after work hours.

Had some doors opened that I thought should have been opened, I do not believe I would have been able to focus on this dream project. My time and attention before and after work hours would have had to be focused on other things and I would have worn myself out. I can honestly say I am happy for the person that got the job and it was just not meant for me, it was not my time or place. God had other things in mind for me to concentrate on. Things to further the kingdom, things that lined up with my gifts and talents. Things that allowed me to not be stressed and gave me peace and enjoyment in life. Now I was thanking God that the job I wanted so badly was not my destiny. I would have missed out on so much more from life.

As a manager I was given the opportunity to work remotely which allowed my over ambitious self to work for my job as well as help take care of my father, continue my Adjunct Professor teaching at a University, formally establish the "family business", complete my dream house project, expand our family real estate business and document our current and future philanthropic endeavors before and after work hours from my day job. I think if I did get that other position it would not have been right for me and my ultimate purpose in life. I am now very very thankful for that closed door.

Chapter 26

I once had a boss that told me I would never be able to write or finish my Bachelor's degree. I would hear him talk about me so badly through his office walls. He was hard of hearing and did not realize how loud he spoke. Imagine if I had actually believed him and never tried to complete my degree. You have to be able to filter out these negative things that people say to you. Not only was I able to finish my Bachelor's degree but I obtained a Master of Science in Health Care Administration and a Master of Science in Management Information Systems as well as I wrote this book. I say this to brag on how God can make your crooked places straight and how with determination you can accomplish your goals. God knows what is best for your life and we have to be thankful for the opened doors as well as the closed doors.

The dream house and estate that was built is not financed, and is 100% owned outright. It took 20 years from inception to completion, however 10 of those years were tied up in court with my maternal Uncles. I really believe they thought they would wear me down, but I always said that they were not fighting me and that battle was not mine for sure, it was God's plan that had to come to fruition. I was given strength and tenacity to endure the struggle.

Nowadays my family and I frequent Grenada many times during the year and are able to enjoy the house and lovely grounds. I was so happy to recently be able to take my dad to Grenada to be able to see what all the fuss was about over the years.

Some people have come into my life at various parts of the chapters within my life. If they came into my life during the blessing when the house was completed, they judge me by the blessing, but they never got to see my ashes. They never saw the times when I was trying to figure out how to begin to design the house and pay for the design in installments or how to build the foundation, and roof. At times we were the janitors, housekeepers and the painters and gardeners, even the plumber and electrician. Standing behind the finish product are my mother's prayers and my father's prayers as well as the prayers of my loved ones and true friends. I always say if in life you find a few true and good friends, then you have done well.

~

Write the vision and make it plain on tablets,

That he may run who reads it. For the vision is yet for an appointed time; But at the end it will speak, and it will not lie. Though is tarries, wait for it; because it will surely come, Habakkuk 2

This journey that I have been on has been nothing less than a roller coaster of emotions, trials and tests that ultimately have become my testimony. This journey will hopefully help others know that if you stay focused and behave purposefully while in faith that "with God all things are possible." Matthew 19:26

We all have a purpose in this life. Part of my purpose is for others to see and know to NEVER GIVE UP on your dreams. Trust God and he will bring you through to your purpose. It may not happen how you want it to happen, but it will make you stronger, wiser and be a witness for the kingdom.

The process of building the dream house has been a challenge. However it has been a faith builder and rewarding to see it completed without a mortgage.

The hurts are in the past and I am now able to see I am Blessed, with Beauty for Ashes, double for my trouble, in Jesus name. To God be the glory for the things he has done. Amen.

The End

Isiah 61:3

To console those who mourn in Zion, To give them beauty for ashes, The oil of joy for mourning, The garment of praise for the spirit of heaviness; That they may be called trees of righteousness, The planting of the Lord, that he may be glorified.

About the Author

Sandra E. E. Williams was born in the Caribbean, lives in the United States and enjoys traveling around the world with her husband Kevin Williams. She is a devoted wife and the proud parent of five college graduates. She is a devout Christian whose goal is to make a positive meaningful impact to the lives of others through motivational, mentoring and philanthropic endeavors. By profession, Sandra has been in the field of Information Technology for over 30 years. Sandra is founder, CEO and co-owner of Williams Estate vacation rental property and a real estate investor in collaboration with her husband. Sandra earned a Master of Science degree in Management Information Systems, and a Master of Science degree in Health Care Administration from Wilmington University, where she is also an Adjunct Professor. Sandra also earned a Bachelor of Science degree in Business Administration from Wesley College.